On Refugees

To be called a refugee is the opposite of an insult; it is a badge of strength, courage, and victory.
 —Tennessee Office for Refugees

No one puts their children in a boat unless the water is safer than the land.
 —Warsan Shire

A refugee is someone who survived and who can create the future.
 —Amela Koluder

Refugees are not terrorists. They are often the first victims of terrorism.
 —António Manuel de Oliveira Guterres

The world will not be destroyed by those who do evil, but by those who watch them without doing anything.
 —Albert Einstein

Give me your tired, your poor, your huddled masses yearning to breathe free.
 —Emma Lazarus

No one leaves home unless home is the mouth of a shark.
 —Warsan Shire

Refugees are mothers, fathers, sisters, brothers, children, with the same hopes and ambitions as us—except that a twist of fate has bound their lives to a global refugee crisis on an unprecedented scale.
 —Khaled Hosseini

We have a legal and moral obligation to protect people fleeing bombs, bullets and tyrants, and throughout history those people have enriched our society.
 —Juliet Stevenson

"It is the obligation of every person born in a safer room to open the door when someone in danger knocks.
 —Dina Nayeri

Denise Smith had just returned from six years with her husband and their [missionary work] in Beirut. She pondered and prayed on what meaning her life might take when her church . . . called her and asked if she would come speak to a group of refugee women, most of whom only spoke Arabic.

She agreed and began to ponder and pray on what she could offer them. The plan revealed itself in her trusty old sewing machine. "I took it everywhere with me," says Denise. "I am never without it."

That first meeting began a journey that became the answer to many prayers. The prayers of women who have fled horrific conditions and only want one small opportunity to make a living, raise good children and BE American, as well as the prayers of a woman who wanted to know what she should do with herself. Peace of Thread was born of these prayers.

The designer accessories company [Peace of Thread] provides training, language lessons, fellowship and jobs for women who have made their way from upheaval and threat to a place they can breathe and make a new life out of the patches of their former selves.
—*GwinnetCitizen.com*

Holt captures the stories of refugees—as well as the volunteers who served them: people who became true heroes despite distressing circumstances in their lives. The stories are authentic and unfiltered, and tell of each person's intimate life and struggles. I felt the pain in each story, and I was rewarded by the love, kindness, and hope that resurrected.
—Angela Khoury
   Board Member, Alif Institute, Atlanta, Ga

Peace of Thread weaves together the moving narratives of courageous women whose journeys brought them to Clarkston—a little town with a big heart. My eyes filled with tears of pride.
—Edward "Ted" Terry
   Mayor, Clarkston, Ga

Holt shows how Denise Smith lives out her compassion for refugee women seeking support and for American women volunteers with the courage to move beyond their comfort zone. Her strength, drive, love, and grit have made Peace of Thread the success it is today.
   —Erin Burchik
      children's book author and founder of the Joy Market, Ga

Holt gives an inspiring account of how one person has transformed the lives of many refugee women. By Denise Smith's example, we are challenged to personally reach out to the newcomers among us.
   —Bobby King
      Refugee Family Services (retired), Atlanta

In a world full of heartache, we need more folks like those in Peace of Thread who truly care for and love the poor, the infirm, the dispossessed, while expecting nothing in return. This approach opens a door. It reaches those in need, helps to fulfill physical, emotional, and spiritual needs. To love our neighbors as ourselves. This is what is required for the long term change desperately needed around the globe.
   —Mary Stanley, Founder
      The Fancy Feather (NGO), Pluma Hidalgo, Oaxaca, Mexico

The subject of displaced people is timely, and Holt's insight into the journey of refugees from their famine stricken or war torn countries to resettlement in the USA is very important for our fellow citizens. We should read these stories. We should learn from these lives.
   —Rev Dr Fahed Abu-Akel, Presbytery of Greater Atlanta
      Founder of Atlanta Ministry with International Students

In a time when few seem to agree on what to do with our immigration crisis, Denise Smith has an answer. That answer is formed in the value and hope she sees in each person, whether a refugee or a volunteer who serves refugees, that her life has touched in the last eight years. That answer is pieced together with a mix of reclaimed materials and reclaimed lives. Peace of Thread does more than produce works of beauty, it produces dignity.
   —Randy Ezra Rainwater
      Pastor Grace New Hope

For my family and for the refugees of Clarkston

Empower a Refugee

Peace of Thread & the Backyard Humanity Movement

Patricia Martin Holt

Becky,

Make a Difference!

Always,

Pat

❮❶❯Cune

Empower a Refugee:
Peace of Thread and the Backyard Humanity Movement
by Patricia Martin Holt
© 2020 Patricia Martin Holt
Cune Press, Seattle 2020
First Edition

Paperback   ISBN 9781951082666 $16.00

For the Library of Congress CIP information for
Empower a Refugee, please contact Cune Press:
www.cunepress.com

Credit:
Cover photo by Sebastian Rich: sebastianrichphotography.com.
Quotations on Refugees, page 1: compiled by Global Giving.
www.globalgiving.org.

Quotation on page 2 is from GwinnetCitizen.com (Jan 7, 2015).

Bible Citations are from the King James translation (public domain)
and from the New Living Bible Translation copyright 2015 by Tyndale House Foundation. Tyndale House Publishers, Inc.

For other credits, see the Acknowledgement.

 Bridge Between the Cultures (a series from Cune Press)

Leaving Syria	Bill Dienst & Madi Williamson
Turning Fear Into Power	Linda Sartor
Visit the Old City of Aleppo	Khaldoun Fansa
Steel & Silk	Sami Moubayed
Syria - A Decade of Lost Chances	Carsten Wieland
The Road from Damascus	Scott C. Davis
A Pen of Damascus Steel	Ali Ferzat
White Carnations	Musa Rahum Abbas
Apartheid Is a Crime	Mats Svensson
Stories My Father Told Me	Helen Zughaib & Elia Zughaib

Contents

To the Reader by Rita Zawaideh   8
Jesus Speaks to His Disciples   11
1   Transitions: A World of Possibilities   13
2   Najah: Grateful to Be Home Again   17
3   Denise & Art: Lifetime Guarantee   27
4   Peace of Thread: Born in the USA   39
5   Emain: Take Care of My Son   55
6   Denise's Circles: Comfort, Care, & Commitment   62
7   Fahima: I Learned to Drive   79
8   Nasima: The Price of Education   84
9   Memphis: New Threaders, New Patterns   91
10 Clarkston: One Square Global Mile   104
Epilogue   112

Resources
Endnotes   114
Appendix   118
Further Reading   120

Acknowledgments   122
Index   123
Cune Press   126
The Author   128

To the Reader

Jordanian-born Rita Zawaideh now does humanitarian work from her base in Seattle.

In a world and a national media environment where truth is a rare commodity, Americans like Patricia Martin Holt occasionally stand forth as truth tellers. If we are to heal our divisions, solve the most pressing problems with our economy, and recover our humanity . . . we would do well to read *Empower a Refugee* by Patricia Martin Holt and to study the Peace of Thread organization that it documents.

Patricia Martin Holt first experienced the ennobling effect of working with refugees (and, specifically of using fabric projects to create a future for women refugees) when her husband was posted to Amman, Jordan and she met Leila Wahbeh, an amazing local woman who was serving Palestinian refugees. Later, in the Atlanta area, she discovered Peace of Thread, a project started by another renaissance woman, Denise Smith. Peace of Thread taught fabric skills, provided sewing machines, fabric, workspace, and gave refugee women a commercial outlet for their work. Peace of Thread has inspired other Americans to work with refugees as well as with the poor and disadvantaged. It is now opening chapters in other locations in the US.

What truths do *Empower a Refugee* and Peace of Thread tell us?

First, refugees are not statistics or news items. They are people just like us. They are mothers and fathers, young children, teenagers, grandmothers—the entire gamut of our humanity is reflected in who refugees are.

Refugees are part of the solution to our greatest national problems. Our birth rate is declining, our workforce participation rate has fallen off a cliff, even the French do a better job of keeping middle-aged males working productively in the labor force. Our labor markets are very very tight and our

GDP cannot grow freely unless more workers are available. How to pay for infrastructure? How to pay our teachers? How to pay the costs of responding to climate change? What of the costs of health care?

The German Prime Minister Angela Merkel opened the doors wide to Syrian refugees in August, 2015, allowing more than a million to flood into the country. Her motive? Reuters referred to "Germany's shrinking labour force" and its "aging population."

"Government officials see [Merkel's immigration] law, which is welcomed by employers, as a game-changer in the global race for talent since other countries are espousing stricter immigration rules."*

The hard fact is that Germany needs to renew its workforce if its economy is to avoid collapse. France, Britain, and to a lesser extent the US are facing the same challenge.

Yes, when refugees first arrive in a host country they require some assistance to get settled and to find a niche in the economy. But their children and grandchildren are overwhelmingly stable, productive, solid contributors to the economy and culture of their adoptive countries. And many of them become notables, strivers, shot out of a cannon: women and men who can spark a cascade of benefits to society.

And how do refugees help those of us in the host nation to recover our soul? Patricia Martin Holt, the refugee workers she met in Jordan, and the volunteers and staff at Peace of Thread speak of the ennobling effect of assisting other human beings in a time of need.

Working with refugees in the US, Britain, Germany—all over the world—brings out our humanity. It enables us to become our best version of ourselves.

Rita Zawaideh has helped to resettle refugees in the Seattle area for many years. Her non-profit SCM-Medical Missions / Salaam Cultural Museum also works internationally to bring "relief and aid to people affected by conflict and natural disaster within the Middle East and North Africa" and is currently building schools and delivering education and medical services to refugees in Greece.

For more: www.scmmedicalmissions.org or www.salaamculturalmuseum.org or on facebook: scm medical missions

Reuters World News: "Merkel takes a gamble with new immigration law" by Micael Nienaber. September 18, 2018

Jesus Speaks to His Disciples

[In this passage Jesus refers to himself in the Holy Bible passage below as the "Son of Man" and also as the "King."]

But when the Son of Man comes in his glory, and all the angels with him, then he will sit upon his glorious throne. All the nations will be gathered in his presence, and he will separate the people as a shepherd separates the sheep from the goats. He will place the sheep at his right hand and the goats at his left.

Then the King will say to those on his right, "'Come, you who are blessed by my Father, inherit the Kingdom prepared for you from the creation of the world. For I was hungry, and you fed me. I was thirsty, and you gave me a drink. I was a stranger, and you invited me into your home. I was naked, and you gave me clothing. I was sick, and you cared for me. I was in prison, and you visited me."

Then these righteous ones will reply, "Lord, when did we ever see you hungry and feed you? Or thirsty and give you something to drink? Or a stranger and show you hospitality? Or naked and give you clothing? When did we ever see you sick or in prison and visit you?"

And the King will say, "I tell you the truth, when you did it to one of the least of these my brothers and sisters, you were doing it to me!"

Then the King will turn to those on the left and say, "Away with you, you cursed ones, into the eternal fire prepared for the devil and his demons. For I was hungry, and you didn't feed me. I was thirsty, and you didn't give me a drink. I was a stranger, and you didn't invite me into your home. I was naked, and you didn't give me clothing. I was sick and in prison, and you didn't visit me."

Then they will reply, "Lord, when did we ever see you hungry or thirsty or a stranger or naked or sick or in prison, and not help you?"

And he will answer, "I tell you the truth, when you refused to help the least of these my brothers and sisters, you were refusing to help me."

—Matthew 25: 3-45

Artisan Threader

Transitions:
A World of Possibilities

You must not oppress foreigners. You know what it's like to
be a foreigner, for you yourselves were once foreigners in the
land of Egypt.
            —Exodus 23:9

IN 1982, I CLOSED MY BUSINESS AND TRAVELED TO AMMAN, Jordan, to
join my husband, who was stationed there on a consulting assignment.
While he was working, I had the luxury to indulge my lifelong interest in
arts and crafts. As I explored the city's shops, I became captivated by the
counted cross-stitch textiles I saw for sale. Soon I met Leila Wahbeh,[1] who
was my entrée to the artists—women living in Palestinian refugee camps in
and around Amman. These camps had been established to provide refuge to
Palestinians expelled or displaced from their homes in the 1948 Arab-Israeli
War [2]. Palestinian women had continued their traditional embroidery practice
since their displacement.

With each visit to the camps, my understanding of hardship greatly
expanded. Here were families who had lost everything—penniless yet
generous with hospitality, holding fast to dignity and hope amid a landscape
of cement block shelters with corrugated metal roofs and narrow dirt roads.
Before long, I recognized that the loss I witnessed applied to victims of war
and chaos worldwide. My eyes opened to all displaced people, especially the
women and children, trapped as if behind bars.

Thirty years later my husband had died, and I was living in Atlanta,
Georgia. A short drive away, in Clarkston, I found a large and diverse refugee
resettlement program. Hoping to volunteer on behalf of refugees, I contacted
several local agencies. My search led me to Denise Smith and Peace of Thread,
a nonprofit she had founded. Denise and a team of volunteers were teaching
refugee women to sew one-of-a-kind, artisan handbags using donated sewing
machines and fabrics. Immediately, I was hooked on their work and their story.

I learned that in 1997, Denise and her husband Art had lost their teenage
son and other close relatives. Grieving and exhausted, they sought a change
of scene, which they found working in the mountains of Lebanon. For six

years, Denise and Art served a Christian organization's staff and volunteers who in turn served villagers in the Middle East. When she and her husband returned to the Atlanta area, Denise used the skill in speaking Arabic she had acquired abroad to engage with refugee mothers in Clarkston. She sought to continue the fellowship she'd enjoyed with families in the mountains where she and Art had lived.

As Denise and then Art came to know Clarkston's refugee families, their innate desire to serve inevitably emerged. Too often, resettled refugees find themselves isolated rather than enjoying a new life in which family, friends, work, and affinity groups interweave to create a true home. Denise met refugee women unable to work due to language and other barriers but eager to connect to their new community and contribute to their families. Accomplished at sewing, Denise offered to teach the women to sew, and from her initial offer, Peace of Thread was born. The enterprise helps women empower themselves and regain a sense of purpose. The project in Clarkston later sparked an offshoot in Memphis, Tennessee. Art now teaches nights at a trade school for refugee men near Peace of Thread. Through their attention to their refugee neighbors, the Smiths have been a force behind a network of assistance that complements the services of refugee resettlement agencies and local organizations.

This book recounts the story of Peace of Thread: the founders and volunteers who make its work possible, and the Afghan, Iraqi, Myanmar, Somali, and Congolese women whose lives, uprooted by conflict and persecution, have been supported by the project. These women had lost family members, homes, and support systems. They arrived in the United States—sometimes after living years in limbo—with an imperfect knowledge of English and misunderstandings of American culture. Within the embrace of Denise Smith and a circle of volunteers, the refugee women learned a wealth of new skills and became, once again, contributing members of their families as well as vital members of their US communities.

To understand what drives the people behind Peace of Thread, and to learn about the families that benefit from the organization, I spoke with a range of people whose language skills vary widely. Some people in this story are native speakers of English. For other interviewees, English is a second or third language, and their level of proficiency spans basic to fluent. To interview a few of the refugee women, I engaged the help of bilingual interpreters.

In retelling the experiences of these diverse contributors, I've tried to preserve their individual voices and points of view. I've structured the book to allow for multiple voices and to give emphasis to life-defining events. In the chapters devoted to refugee women, I convey their stories as they told them to me. Because the lives of many of these refugees and those of their families remain endangered, I use their first names only, and in some cases, I've changed their names and the immediate locations in which selected events occurred. In the chapters about the founders of Peace of Thread and their networks, I use my own voice to clarify and advance the information they shared with me. In all cases, I've made every effort not to alter or distort the substance of the individuals' experiences. I am awed by the bravery and fortitude of all the people who contributed their life events to this book. And I am deeply appreciative of all the people who opened their hearts to me and recounted sensitive and painful times.

I've reflected on how complicated we sometimes think it is to make a difference in the lives of people less fortunate than we are. We seek out projects half-a-world away from our homes and make enormous investments of time and money. I believe such projects are vital, but at the same time, I fear we may overlook how we can contribute to the local quality of life in small ways, through actions that take only small investments of time and are nearly cost-free. My hope is that the stories in this book will inspire individuals, small groups, and nonprofits everywhere to look around and start from home in opening a vast world of possibilities for others and ourselves.

Artisan Threaders at Work

Najah:
Grateful to Be Home Again

The women of Moab are left like homeless birds
at the shallow crossings of the Arnon River.
"Help us," they cry.
"Defend us against our enemies.
Protect us from their relentless attack.
Do not betray us now that we have escaped.
Let our refugees stay among you.
Hide them from our enemies until the terror is past."
    —Isaiah 16:2-4

WHO ARE THE REFUGEE WOMEN WHO WORK WITH PEACE OF THREAD? I heard volunteers mention one refugee woman—Najah—who had learned to sew with Denise Smith, the nonprofit's founder, and then graduated to a position teaching other refugee women.

After living in a Clarkston apartment for several years, Najah and her family moved to a home of their own. Najah passed a driving test and drove locally with confidence. Hers was a success story I wanted to hear. I wondered about her early life and transition to adulthood. What had she endured in her native country that had caused her to seek refugee status?

I met with Najah in her home, a pleasant blend of Iraqi and American cultures and styles. A Muslim woman, Najah observed the practice of wearing a headscarf in public as a sign of modesty. In the privacy of her home, however, her long, ash-blonde hair need not be covered. She greeted me with a warm smile and said, "You are welcome."

She wore a floor-length pink dress with silver filigree that complemented her fair skin. Her backless shoes, easy to remove when kneeling for prayer, clicked against a tile floor as she led me to the living room where she had set out hot tea, baklava, wafer cookies, and chunks of watermelon.

After a cup of tea and a treat, she settled back on the sofa and began. In a deep melodic voice, she told me her story, the story of a middle-class girl in a traditional culture where the rules of behavior are very different from ours. Najah's culture offered extended family, stability, and the security of knowing that following the rules maintains a woman's place in society. When political unrest began to sweep across Iraq, Sunni Muslims like Najah and her family were among the groups for whom life became precarious. This is what Najah told me.

"After my grandmother's first husband died, she married another man. At the time, she had three daughters—my mother and her two sisters. I never knew this husband wasn't my real grandfather. My mother told me that when she was a little girl, he carried her everywhere on his shoulder. He couldn't pass by a flower without stopping to pick it for her. When my mother spoke of him, she said she had loved him.

"My grandfather could read and write and worked for the government. He wore a suit and the title *effendi*. He worked with road construction in the north of the country. When he came home, he brought a monthly report with the names of all the workers and what they did, and the office gave him money to pay them. On the day of the office visit, he would take my mother with him and tell my grandmother not to cook. He would bring dinner home from a shop.

"In the summer, my grandparents were alone, so my mother sent me or my sister to visit them and give them company. My grandfather often went to the warm springs near the river to swim. To get there, he took public transportation and walked. One day when he was eighty-five or ninety years old, he got tired and fell. People passing by asked if he needed help. He couldn't speak, so they took him to a hospital close to the springs. We didn't have a phone, so when he didn't come home, my uncle went to the hospital and asked if anyone had received an old man. He told them my grandfather's name, and the staff said, 'We have his body.'

"I was nine years old when my grandfather died. After several days I saw him in heaven, sitting in a bed. He always wore pajamas—*always*, but on this day, he wore a short *dishdasha*. I said, 'How are you, grandfather?' He said, 'I'm good. Truly, now I am good.'

"My mother and father married in 1948 when she was seventeen and he was twenty-one. My father and his brother left for Palestine right after the wedding to fight with the Arab Army against Israel. He returned home just before my oldest brother, the first child, was born.

"My mother had sixteen children. Four were lost to death. My oldest brother drowned in the river near the springs. Two brothers died by age three of disease. The fourth brother died right after birth. I was in the middle of eight brothers and three sisters.

"My father had two wives. My mother was his first wife, and the second wife was not much younger. My mother didn't accept this arrangement, so our families lived in separate houses. In general, we love each other, but even brothers sometimes have problems. My mother was Kurdish, the other woman Arab Iraqi.[1] We say race, tribe, location. My mother-in-law, for example, is Turkmen,[2] but still Iraqi. My brothers and sisters are still in Iraq, and I have tribes in Jordan and Syria as well.

"The big mistake for Iraq was going into Kuwait.[3] Before then, Iraqis didn't pay taxes. I went to school for free to become a teacher, and my husband finished college. Three of my brothers are engineers. If you were smart, you could get a master's or doctoral degree for free. When you finished college, you could put your name on a list for a brand new car from Europe or Asia or South America, and there were no taxes or insurance costs. My mother received a new eye from a donor, and the surgery was in a clean, modern hospital where she was served three meals a day. Jobs were plentiful, and people had shops to sell plates or handicrafts. When I was five and six years old, I would go out at night to sell yogurt we made using milk from our cow. There was no danger.

"We sided with [Iraqi leader] Hussein in the Iran-Iraq War.[4] We heard in the news that some Iranians who supported the Shah[5] ran from Iran to just inside the border of Iraq and stayed there. They wanted to fight Khomeini, and Hussein put a small camp in Iraq for those people. Government employees included people who were Shia, Sunni, Kurdish, Christian, and from other groups. In my brother's neighborhood, there is a huge apartment building where Palestinians live, and my oldest sister has Palestinian friends. My husband has many Shia friends, even though we are Sunni.

"My husband's aunt—his mother's sister-in-law—lived in the house behind ours. She was a poor widow who took care of her children by operating a store in her house. We want to help widows, so my mother went to her store to buy tomatoes, okra, and garlic. She sent the children to buy something—Pepsi, ice cream. It was easy to live in our country; life was simple. We walked to school, to the hospital. My oldest sister had a store in her house too, and she understood business. The neighbors would say, 'School is starting. Please bring the things we need.' She sold clothes, school uniforms, books, notebooks, pens, and pencils. We liked being together. Our relatives lived with us or near us. When we marry we stay in the same neighborhood. Of course, if a husband's job takes you away, you must go.

"My husband's mother asked her sister-in-law to find a good family, a

Artisan Trainer Najah

beautiful lady, for her son. The aunt said, 'We have a beautiful girl and a good family right here.' She knew that two of my sisters were already married and that I was now the oldest [unmarried daughter]. You always prepare the oldest girl for marriage first.[6]

"My in-laws-to-be first came to our house to visit in 1984. When their son, Ahmed, came home from his job in another town, his parents said, 'We went to see a family with girls.' Ahmed asked, 'What is their name? What is their brother's name?' When they told him, he said, 'I know this family. I've been in their house. I go to work with their brother.'

"One of my brothers is an aeronautical engineer who graduated after five years in Russia. Ahmed was also an engineer. Their work was hours away, and because Ahmed's house was close to ours, he and my brother traveled to work together.

"Ahmed's parents came to our house again, this time with Ahmed. I went into the room with Ahmed's family and said, 'Hello. How are you?' Then the family talked. Ahmed tried to look at me, and I tried to look at him. I finished serving tea. A glance from my brother told me not to leave the room. I said a few words. I was nervous and confused, and Ahmed was shy too.

"His parents didn't say yes or no. I thought maybe they didn't like me, maybe both families will say no. Maybe if they saw a love story between cousins who knew each other, they might say yes at that moment, but we were not acquainted with each other nor related. After tea for one and a half hours, his parents asked me simple questions about my work and my life and what I like to do. They wanted to introduce themselves to me, get to know me, and know how I act.

"The next day, Ahmed's family called to say, 'We go now to buy the rings and jewelry.' So my brother asked me, 'What do you say? Do you say yes?' I said, 'As you like.'[7] I had been approached by suitors from the time I was fourteen years old, so I had met a lot of men before Ahmed. I always said no. I didn't like their job, I didn't like their face. They were weak, too skinny, not right. I was twenty when I met Ahmed. My mother said, 'Okay. He's from a good family, he finished college, he has a good salary.' My family could say no, they have the right to say no. But when I agreed, my brother said, 'He is good. I know him. I know he is a good man.' I asked about his family. My brother said, 'Good people. His family is good.' We asked about honor. Nothing was bad.

"We became engaged in April 1984 and married that September. During our engagement, Ahmed came to my family's house. We spent time together and ate together. I took some of my family and his oldest sister to get makeup and shoes. Ahmed was in France for work and bought my wedding gown there. He told the saleslady in the store, 'She is beautiful and has a tiny waist. I want the perfect dress for her.' My family gave me gold bracelets and two pairs of earrings, and my mother-in-law bought me short and long gold necklaces.[8]

"Before the engagement party and the wedding, we went to marriage court to obtain our official paper from a religious judge, according to Islamic law. Families go to court because the judge reads part of the holy Qur'an to them. A woman can't get married without a father or brother present if she is a virgin. If not, the judge must see a certificate that she is divorced or a widow. Even then, we like to have a brother or father present.

"The marriage judge asks both families if they agree to the marriage. He asked Ahmed's family, 'Do you have the dowry?' When they said yes, Ahmed gave me money and gold. Already I had chosen, and Ahmed had paid for, furniture, clothes, makeup, and a big television for our room. The Holy Qur'an says my husband must support me if we get divorced. Then it is my right to have a place to go, and my husband must feed and clothe me.[9]

"The judge said, 'Do you, Najah, agree? Do you give the order to your brother to speak for you?'

'Yes,' I said, 'my brother will speak for me.'

"The judge has to be sure the woman agrees. When I agreed, the judge covered Ahmed's and my brother's hands with a white handkerchief. The white means we start with no cheating or lies. We are clean and honest. Two male witnesses must sign the marriage paper. Then we read the Al-Fatiha, the first Surah, which is the first prayer in the Qur'an. We were congratulated with the word *mabrook*. All this must be done before the wedding.

"In our country, the man pays for the wedding. The woman's family has a small engagement party for everyone in both families and with maybe four or five of the bride's friends. Ahmed has five sisters and three sisters-in-law. My mother has eight sisters-in-law. About fifty people from both families came to my party.

"The night before the wedding, the bride has a party for women, and henna is painted on her hands. The party was at our house, but these days, the parties are at public places. Throughout the evening, I wore gowns of different colors. Suddenly, our festive mood ended when someone came to our house to announce that Ahmed's cousin had died. My mother and father had to notify everyone there would be no wedding the next day. We were in shock. We were sad and angry that Ahmed had lost a family member.

"After a death, some people wait ten days, some forty days. In the war between Iran and Iraq, when an Iraqi died, people who wanted to marry would go to the family of the deceased, apologize, and ask the family for forgiveness for wishing to marry. People would say, 'We are sorry for your loss, but we want our son to marry.' The family might answer, 'It's okay, go.' Some families say, 'We will come to your wedding. We will be with you.' Out of respect for the family of the deceased, the wedding is toned down. If Ahmed had asked his family, they would have said not now. He knew his mother wanted a seven-day party because he was the last son. On the seventh day, there is a celebration of marriage at the groom's house, usually just for the women, and guests bring gifts.

"Ahmed waited three days after the death of his cousin to come to get me and take me to his family's house. He brought my wedding dress, carrying it over his arm. He said, 'A woman has one day in her life to wear her white dress.' I put it on and went with him.

"It was night and quiet. No one greeted us, no one prepared a feast. I was so disappointed and hurt that no one hugged me and told me I was welcome. My mother-in-law was taking a bath; she'd just come home from the funeral. When she greeted us, Ahmed said to her, 'I don't care about a celebration. I want my wife.' Then I realized he hadn't told anyone I was coming.

"His mother prepared a big meal for us. That was our celebration, and then I was Ahmed's wife. We had our own room but shared the rest of the house with his family. It is normal in our culture for families to live together. If a wife says she wants a separate house and the man can't provide that, he tells her she is free to go back to her family. Most wives understand and don't ask or stop complaining. We stayed at Ahmed's family's home for a month and then moved to another city for his work. We came home for visits every month and stayed in our room until we bought a house in our home city.

"Wives can work. I was an elementary school teacher. We had no children for thirteen years. My father-in-law loved me because I took good care of Ahmed, but he said, 'We want her to have a baby. If only she would have a baby.' His saying that hurt me so much. The culture imposes a lot of pressure. In fact, there was so much pressure on me that I found another woman for Ahmed, one I thought could bear a child. Ahmed was engaged to this woman for several weeks but came to realize this second marriage would create an even bigger problem than not having children. He said to me, 'We will not do this. We will stay together, and I want only you. I don't want another wife.' When Ahmed broke the engagement with the other woman, I stopped teaching. At the time, all imports and exports were stopped to punish Hussein for entering Kuwait.[10] The sanctions made it hard for Iraqis because we could sell only a little bit of oil and there was inflation. For me, it wasn't worth working because my monthly salary was cut so much I couldn't even afford shoes. People were selling their furniture just to survive.

"After five miscarriages, I had my first child in 1997, then three years later, my second child. All went along until 2003, when rebel forces bombed our house. It was a ground bomb that blew out the windows and the door. We were afraid. We left the house with a few clothes and moved to our in-laws. Shortly after, we left their house and rented a house nearby. I had just learned I was pregnant with my third child.

"We left Iraq in 2004 when our baby was a month old. We knew if we were attacked again we might not survive. We told no one, not our families, not our friends, no one. At five in the morning on September 27, we drove to Amman, Jordan, without incident, and we thanked God. Militias were everywhere, stopping people, and looking at their ID cards. If a man had a Sunni name, they shot him and his family where they stood.

"We thought we would be away from Iraq for a short time, so we moved into a furnished apartment in a good area of Amman. As time went on, we had to move to cheaper and cheaper places. We weren't allowed to work in Jordan, and the paperwork to come to the United States took so long, we were running out of money. The boys were five and seven by then and couldn't be in our bedroom, so they slept on the floor in the living room. Survival became so hard we had to ask relatives in Iraq to send us clothes. Ahmed became more and more sad. He was used to making decisions and caring for us; now he was helpless.

"In Jordan, we learned that insurgents had killed my brother and my nephews. They killed Ahmed's twin brother, two of his nephews, and two of his cousins. Some victims were intentionally killed on the first of Ramadan or Eid[11] so that people would have nothing to celebrate. On the first day of Eid, rebels went to my aunt's house and grabbed her only son and her grandson. She followed them into the street and begged for their lives. Everyone was crying and screaming, but their cries were ignored. Finally she begged them to spare at least one. The rebels took them five minutes from the house, shot her son, stabbed her grandson, and left them to die on the street. If families try to remove bodies for burial, the rebels shoot them. They want the bodies to rot.

"As time went on, month after month, year after year, we went through all the stages of grief to finally accepting the situation. Jobless, feeling the future did not include us, we continued struggling to find a way to leave Jordan. No matter how bad things became, we knew if we were in Iraq, we wouldn't survive. It was far too dangerous to return home, and even if it were safe, my husband would never find a job that would match his expertise.

"There is a saying in our country, 'If you eat the sweet, you must eat the sour.' I had a really good life with my husband back home. We love each other. From the first day I was with him, he allowed me to visit my friends. He took me on vacation each year. He supported me and loved me. How could I not stand with him during a hard time?

"Two months after we left home, rebels took over the whole area, but we told each other it could be worse. In Amman, a charitable organization took us to a restaurant for a meal during Ramadan. My children could go to the zoo for thirty-five US cents. We had a large Iraqi refugee community for support. People offered free computer classes and art and music classes for adults and children. Three months before we left Amman, my husband was offered a job there. Why didn't it happen sooner?

"Ahmed knew someone who had told him to go to the International Organization for Migration. He did, and then the paperwork moved more quickly than it had before. Finally, after five years in Jordan, we were accepted to come the United States, and we left on January 15, 2009. We had hoped for

Europe, because if rebels learn that a family has gone to the United States, they say the family is not loyal to their own country, and they shoot the family members who stay behind.

"When we arrived in the United States, we were taken to Decatur[12] by a refugee agency and put into a small apartment. Ahmed could speak English, but the children and I could speak only a little English. We had no car, no job, no furniture, nothing. We lived in Decatur for a while then moved to an apartment in Clarkston. Ahmed applied for many jobs but was not hired. Then a neighbor called and said a property management company wanted to talk to him. Ahmed was offered a job as manager of one of the apartment properties. Now Ahmed manages twelve of the many properties the company owns. He succeeded in this business.

"One day, about three years later, Denise [Smith] came to the rental office and spoke to Ahmed about helping refugees. She asked for a place to meet with refugee women, and he gave her the use of a room near the rental office. Refugee women could walk there. When Ahmed told me about Denise and that I could earn money for sewing, I went to be trained. Now I am a trainer at the center, and Denise has become our good friend.

"Denise teaches the refugees to have confidence and to be strong. To live in this country, women must take care of their children and help their husbands with financial support. I was afraid to drive in this city, there's so much traffic. Denise said I must drive if I want to go places during the day. My husband is at work, he can't take me, so now I drive.

"I see this is a land of immigrants. Everywhere I go I see people of many colors. The ones who came before us made it, now it's our turn. I want to support the refugee women. Every time I go to the training center, I make a new friend—a new refugee woman or a new volunteer. There are always new things I can learn, and I like to work with Denise.

"After five years in the United States, we became citizens. In 2016, Ahmed flew to Germany with officials of Atlanta and Clarkston to share our success story with German government officials and refugee aid organizations. They also visited refugee shelters.

"In June 2014, after ten years away, I was able to go home for a visit. I wanted to take our children but couldn't. A crowd of about twenty-five people met me at the airport. I saw my mother; she was then eighty-four and weak. We were always very close to each other. My nieces and nephews were all grown up, and there were children I'd never met.

"I cried when I saw how our neighborhood had changed. Now it's still not safe, but my family has to live there. Where would they go? My oldest brother is sixty-five. It's not easy to change places. There's not enough money to leave now. ISIS[13] takes your money, and many people are out of work. No one is building houses, and there are no government jobs. It is very depressed. College is still free, thank goodness, but people pay for electricity, gas, and transportation.

"I planned to stay for a month and a half, but a bad situation came. ISIS had taken the right part of the city and had destroyed my home, our families' homes. I was staying with my brothers on the left side, changing residences with my mother. Ahmed was concerned for my safety and wanted me to come home. Nothing was happening there yet, but people couldn't go outside, especially at night because of a curfew. Then after a few days, ISIS came to the left side of the city in the early morning. We heard the news because people were texting and calling each other. ISIS is here! They are coming! My brothers told their sons, 'Put your aunt's bags in the car.' We left at 5 a.m. Thousands of people were leaving for North Kurdistan.[14] My oldest sisters and my sister-in-law all left with me with their families.

"I hid my passport, my ID, my plane ticket, everything in my corset. When we got to the border, there were thousands of people. We weren't allowed to cross because the Kurds didn't want us to come in. It was so hot. From five in the morning to five at night, we sat in the heat. Children were crying and screaming. There was no place to sit but in the car or on the street. We had food with us; otherwise, we would have had nothing. At one in the morning, they said if you have relatives in Kurdistan you can cross; otherwise, you will go to a camp. My sister had married her Kurdish cousin and she had the right papers to cover the whole family. Her husband worked in Kurdistan and came home weekends, so they had rented an apartment there.

"I called Ahmed to say I was safe, and I left for the United States a week later. My family was waiting for me at baggage claim when I arrived. I was so excited to see them. Ahmed held a bouquet of flowers. I took the flowers and hugged them all, grateful to be home."

Denise & Art:
Lifetime Guarantee

And if a stranger sojourn with thee in your land, ye shall
not vex him.
But the stranger that dwelleth with you shall be unto you
as one born among you, and thou shalt love him as thyself;
for ye were strangers in the land of Egypt: I am the LORD
your God.
—Leviticus 19:33-34

DENISE SMITH'S COMMITMENT TO SERVING OTHERS started early in life.
As a second grader, she moved with her parents and two older siblings
from Columbus, Ohio, to five acres down a dirt road in the Ohio countryside. While building their country home, the family of five lived in a small
camper, and young Denise helped dig the holes for the outhouse and a fence
around the property.

The move was an early loss for Denise. She left behind the comfort of
her first home and the many relatives—cousins, grandparents, aunts, and
uncles—who lived on her street. Denise remembers a huge change and not
knowing any neighbors, but one thing didn't change at all.

"My life was uncertain," she told me. "My mom and dad were always
yelling at each other, and their arguments didn't end in forgiveness. My father
was a Greyhound bus driver. When he was away, my mom cleaned houses
and ironed and sold encyclopedias. When my dad came home from work,
arguments escalated."

Denise's parents came to their marriage with burdens from large, work-
ing-class families in which alcoholism took a heavy toll. Religion was part of
the family's life, but like so much in Denise's early years, her faith tradition
became complicated.

"In 1959, when I was two years old, my parents left the Catholic Church
for an evangelical church. My dad became Sunday school superintendent,
even though he was never really taught the Bible. Despite religion, Mom and
Dad would have screaming fights on Sunday mornings, which they resumed
when we returned to the car from the sanctuary."

Denise Smith, Founder

Sometimes, Denise's parents' anger wasn't directed solely at each other, and over time, their anger grew to encompass their children.

"Then, when I was a teenager, my dad began drinking and left the faith. He became the town drunk. As I witnessed my parents' behavior, I became certain that escape was my only option."

Denise's route to an independent life wasn't straightforward.

"At fourteen, I went to a summer church camp—as a reprieve from home life and the world around me. It was 1971, a time of unrest, with protests against the war in Vietnam. I went to the camp's church carrying my King James Bible. At the church, a marathon runner spoke using The Living Bible,[1] and suddenly the idea of faith made sense to me.

"When altar calls started, I raised my hand and asked for prayer.[2] I went up to the speaker and asked him to pray for me. He told me to go to my bunk, open my Bible, and ask God to speak.

"I stayed up all night. Home was so loud, I couldn't hear anything, but in the quiet of camp, I could hear myself think."

The peacefulness Denise experienced ended when camp came to an end. She returned home, and the trauma of her life continued.

"Sometimes prostitutes and other women would call. If I answered the phone, they'd tell me how my father hates my mother."

At the time, Denise's older sister, Lynn, was attending nursing school in Miami, Florida.

"For spring break, my parents let me go see Lynn. I was fifteen, and the school in Miami was my introduction to another culture. That visit taught me I had a voice and that I didn't have to be a victim of my family situation any more. I decided the way out was to graduate from high school early and join my sister at her college. I turned sixteen in November, finished high school by July, and for $250, I bought a 1966 white Ford Mustang. I worked all summer as a babysitter and on the night shift at a fast food restaurant. I saved all the money I earned so I could buy the car, and I left for Florida, for a degree in the Bible and psychology.

"I was with my sister, and we did 'beach ministry'—finding people to hang out with and creating conversations outside our comfort zone. To complete my sophomore year, I needed two classes, but the professor who taught them left the school. I took a semester off, worked at a department store, and waited for his replacement. I was stashing money away, and retailing could've been my career. Soon my sister, other nursing students, and I moved off campus to a two-bedroom apartment."

With this move, Denise's journey took another turn: Art Smith, the man she would later marry, established himself in her life. Denise first met Art when she had visited her sister a few years earlier. They spoke a couple of times at the campus swimming pool.

Art, who is four years older than Denise, was Lynn's friend. They had met at the college, where the use of alcohol was forbidden. One day Art was at a hair salon where, for reasons no one remembers, beer was being served. Art had had an earlier spell with drugs and alcohol, but for five years he'd been clean. Someone from the college's student council overheard him say he'd had a beer while having a haircut. The student reported Art to the officials, and he was expelled.

"Art asked Lynn if he could stay at our apartment, and we agreed he could sleep on the couch for a week while he made a plan. When I'd come home from work we'd talk, and a relationship developed.

"On our first date, Art ran into some of his old buddies from drug rehab,"

Denise said. "He introduced me as his fiancée, and when we got back to the car, he announced, 'I'm going to marry you.' I quickly told Art I was looking for *normal*, for a healthy person and a healthy relationship."

Then Denise went away briefly.

"I had developed mononucleosis, and I spent Christmas at the home of a friend whose father was a pastor," Denise said. "He and his wife treated me like a daughter. For the first time, I experienced unconditional love from a father—one who paid enough attention to know how sick I was."

Art kept calling Denise.

"He asked why I wouldn't marry him. He'd quote scripture and tell me what God was sharing with him," Denise explained. "I asked if he could promise he'd never leave me. He said he'd never *want* to leave me, but if he ever stepped out of God's grace, he might not be able to keep his promise. He said, 'I can't promise anything except to pray I never step out of God's grace.'"

Art persisted and went to ask Denise's parents for her hand. He met with no success but continued to pursue Denise.

"He came back to Miami, and on bended knee, again asked to marry me. I had a tug in my heart for a boy in Ohio, but I realized my feelings were infatuation. Love isn't a feeling, it's a commitment," Denise said.

Art and Denise started planning a wedding that Denise's parents tried to undermine. The young couple went to a marriage counselor and said they wanted to elope.

"The counselor stood with us before a justice of the peace in Miami. I was nineteen, and my whole life was about to change."

As husband and wife, Art and Denise moved to Wheaton, Illinois, to live with Art's parents for a while. Art's father was an architect, his mother an operating room nurse. Art had two sisters ten and twelve years older than he, and they had left home long ago. Neither Art nor Denise had graduated college, and they hoped to move to Bloom Township, Ohio, where a wealthy resident had left tuition money for college students. Three months after marrying, however, they found Denise was pregnant.

Art and Denise stayed in Wheaton, where Art went to school during the day and worked nights while Denise worked in restaurants. Later, Art managed an apartment complex.

In 1977, the Smiths' first child, Caleb, was born at home.

"We did a ton of research about at-home birth," Denise said, "and we came to believe it was safest for a baby to enter the world in the environment it had grown in. We wanted our children born without drugs or invasive treatments. Mine was a low-risk pregnancy, and Art was hugely supportive. We read every book we could and got training.

"My sister was a nurse midwife by then, and she came to stay with us and help me through labor. When I reached the last four centimeters before delivery, we invited the local paramedics to come and sit outside our house in case of an emergency. But they didn't need to come in. After the baby was born, they came in to see him and cheer the successful delivery.

"Later, we were contacted by our doctor and midwife and were guests on the Phil Donahue Show in a segment on home births."

The Smiths three children came two years apart—after Caleb, a daughter, Danielle, followed by a son, Jesse.

Art continued his studies, and in January 1981, with his degree in hand, Art shifted his focus to building a long-term career. The family moved to Denver, Colorado, and two years later, to Santa Maria, California. Two years later, they returned to Denver, and after another two years returned to California.

"Art was definitely climbing the corporate ladder," Denise said. "He traveled a lot and was gone from home quite a bit. We moved to New Mexico for a few months, and then finally settled in Orlando, Florida, for about five years."

Denise homeschooled each of her children during their middle school grades, and she supported their involvement in competitive sports. She also worked as a substitute teacher and for a local photographer. All these responsibilities ensured a hectic lifestyle.

"We moved to Atlanta in 1993 for Art's new job in telecommunications. Art and I had been married about seventeen years and had gone through some rocky times. We always went to church, but it was hard for us to get really involved because we moved so much. Art was always working, and we weren't hanging out with the best of people outside of church. Everyone was on the corporate ladder. I was working in children's clothing at a department store, so when Art was traveling I had to get a babysitter to stay with the kids."

This didn't sound to me like the Art and Denise who had brought their children into the world at their own home, surrounded by loved ones.

"We were ready to throw in the towel because nothing was going well. We weren't settled with our commitment, and we needed guidance. We went to a marriage conference in Boulder, Colorado, that saved us. It gave us the tools to make our marriage work."

Back in touch with each other and settled in Atlanta, Art and Denise

Najah at Sales Booth

further strengthened their family when they became involved in Grace Fellowship Church.

"We found Grace through a couple whose house we considered buying," Denise said. "After visiting Grace three times, Art was convinced we would make it our church home."

Key to the Smiths' decision was the church's pastor, Buddy Hoffman, a charismatic and inspiring man who came from a long line of preachers. In February 2017, Buddy died at the age of sixty-three, after having established seven campuses of Grace Fellowship in the Atlanta area. But when Art and Denise joined his church in Lilburn, Georgia, it comprised only about four to five hundred people. In the intimacy the church then offered, the Smiths came to know Buddy well, and over time, their relationship with him and the messages they took from his Bible teaching had a profound influence on the direction their lives would eventually take.

The Smiths' embrace of the church community proved vital because in June 1993 their lives took an unexpected and devastating turn. Art and Denise's youngest son, Jesse, was found to have cancer. During the years of his illness, Jesse was understandably the focus of the Smith family. After his death in 1997, a reconfiguring of family life would ultimately set Art and Denise on an unanticipated journey.

When Jesse was ill, the company Art worked for had been supportive, but after Jesse's death, Art was pressured to move on.

"As an electronics engineer," Art said, "I was responsible for trouble-shooting the design of computer boards. I worked eighty hours a week on a new project, but I couldn't focus. I attributed it to my grief about Jesse. Ten months later, I—along with many others—was laid off."

Art applied for countless jobs and learned about other jobs that were outside of Georgia. At the time, Danielle and Caleb were at a university near Charlotte, North Carolina, and Art couldn't see moving them or being far away from them.

"I had to make a choice," Art said, "unemployment or doing something new. I was always good with my hands, and I started remodeling homes. I found the work therapeutic, and built my own business."

Denise wanted to be a teacher's aide, and she asked her pastor, Buddy, for a reference. Having a sense of what might be therapeutic for Denise, he refused, and instead asked her to run Grace Fellowship's youth department. Along with several church leaders, Denise and Buddy went to visit a church in Florida known to have a successful youth program. The comparable program Denise started at Grace Fellowship soon became hugely successful.

But Denise and Art continued to seek ways to honor Jesse by finding new challenges and serving people in need. In 1999, they made their first mission trip out of the country, a trip their church organized to Costa Rica. This trip started them on an international path.

"We worked with a local church laying the foundation for an orphanage and school in a very poor village," Denise said. "I stirred and poured tons of concrete."

Denise was most interested in the children of the village.

"I saw children who had nothing, yet they were so happy to be alive! They were kind and curious, but there were no schools for them to attend and they didn't have enough to eat. The church provided a hot meal once a day, and there were plans for a playground after the school was built."

Art and Denise followed that trip with other mission trips taken separately or together. At the same time, Denise volunteered in Clarkston with refugee women from Somalia.

"Two friends from Grace Fellowship and I went to an apartment complex to meet with Somali women refugees," Denise said. "We helped them drive, did advocacy work to connect them with services, and offered English classes and after-school programs for their children."

While mulling over their options for work abroad, the Smiths set out for a short-term assignment in Ecuador.

"We wanted to see what some of our missionary friends were doing there," Denise explained. "We went high in the mountains to work at a small school in a village. In the middle of nowhere, I found I could talk about life decisions."

The Smiths told the mission team of their commitment to going somewhere, they just didn't know the time or place. Their children, who were busy with family and career, assured their parents they'd be fine and gave their parents the freedom to explore.

But as Denise, Art, and their children tried to move ahead with their lives, illness again touched the family. Art's father became ill, and in September 2001 Art and Denise settled his parents in the in-law suite attached to a new home they bought east of Atlanta. Then Denise's sister and brother-in-law were in a car accident in Montana, and she went there to care for them. Art's father died while she was gone, and his mother died not long after.

Before then, however, the whole world shook when terrorists who identified themselves with Islam took down the World Trade Center on September 11, 2001.[3] As a result, some Americans sought to distance themselves from other cultures. The approach was different at the Smiths' church. Buddy made the Middle East a priority place for promoting peace and understanding.

First, Buddy convened a team of staff and members from Grace church that traveled to New York City to minister to residents whose lives had been upended by the 9/11 attack. Denise was part of that team.

"Sometimes I was there simply to be a witness to the prayers and memorials family and friends set up for people who were missing," Denise said. "I listened to stories about the people who were lost in the tragedy. Sometimes I would sit quietly with a person in grief or hold someone while she cried. With other members of Grace Fellowship, I went into the pit and handed out cards the children at church had made for the people of New York. I spoke with doormen at apartment buildings whose loss had been forgotten. Life was changed for these men when some residents never came home."

Denise made three service trips to New York City.

"The second and third time, I served in the kitchens next to the pit. My team prepared food for the firemen. I bandaged their feet and put new boots on them. We cleaned rest areas, and we hosted prayer corners. We tried to serve anywhere the Red Cross asked us to."

Buddy further encouraged the members of the church to engage with people from all cultures and nations.

"Buddy challenged us," Denise said. "He asked if we hated Muslims after what we had seen. He made sure we understood they are not the enemy. He made sure we understood the price of bitterness and hate. I met my own hate face on and decided I wanted to love louder than hate."

In between her trips to New York City, Denise's life went on. Earlier, in doing research and making inquiries about serving abroad, Art and Denise had learned about Operation Mobilization, a faith-based organization that works to strengthen communities abroad. A job offer came from the organization, followed by a phone call asking the Smiths to meet with a field leader who was coming through Atlanta from Australia.

"We met with Grant," Art said, "and he told us about an opportunity in Lebanon. He told us what he needed, and we had experience in every area. He wanted vehicles maintained. I could do that. He wanted computers maintained and repaired. I could do that. He wanted the office building maintained. I could do that. He needed someone to run the hospitality house for short-term teams coming into the country. That was right up Denise's alley. He also wanted people who could be like grandparents to the children of the adults on the incoming teams. We were a perfect fit."

Grant told the Smiths he needed someone yesterday and asked for an immediate answer.

"We said yes," Art continued, "even though we didn't have the money we'd need for our airfare and other mission expenses. We'd never intended to move to Lebanon, but we'd always found a way, and this would be no exception."

As Art had sensed, a friend from church called the next day to offer a donation from funds available for benevolent purposes.

"He told me the dollar amount," Art said. "I called the airlines to ask the airfare from Atlanta to Beirut. The cost was the same as the offering from our friend. It was all we needed to move ahead."

"We flew to Lebanon on a ten-day vision trip to make sure we wanted to go there," Denise said. "A young woman from the mission office herded us and our luggage to her car. She was from Germany, but she had been in Lebanon long enough to feel comfortable with the twisting, turning, mountain roads we had to travel to reach the mission office in Aley."

The office, where Art and Denise would eventually work, was the central point for Operation Mobilization's arriving and departing volunteers and employees.

"While I didn't expect luxury, I wasn't prepared for cement floors, a roll-around stove run on propane gas, and no electricity. The office had three bedrooms with two sets of bunk beds and two twin beds, two living areas, a minimal kitchen, and a bath—but no hot water. It was January and miserably cold.

"Our hostess boiled water and served us chicken noodle soup made from packets of dried ingredients, Melba toast, and tea that was stone cold. By candlelight, we found Army blankets. Art observed that I didn't like the place much. I was uncomfortable on so many levels, but exhausted, and I fell asleep.

"We were awakened by angry shouting outside our building. Then someone came in, and we could see a shadow on the door's frosted glass. For a moment, we were convinced someone would report to Operation Mobilization that we'd been found dead, but then the shadow called.

"'Art and Denise. It's Joop! Are you awake? Are you coming out?'

"We peeked out our door to see Joop, another volunteer, jumping up and down to keep warm. He said he was cold and that we had the only heater. He told us that the shouting we'd heard was the vegetable seller using a microphone to alert the villagers to open their pockets.

"Joop was a carpenter who'd lived in the Middle East for many years. He had come to welcome us and help with our breakfast of bread and *zaatar*.[4] Then he took us to see three hospitals, the landscape around us, and Beirut. During our ten-day stay, we met expats from all over Europe, Lebanese people, and hospital personnel. Everyone was kind and hospitable."

One day, a leader from the field office took Art and Denise to Damascus in Syria.[5] At a *souk* [market], Art began a conversation with a young Muslim man that lasted two hours.

"I was shocked at how easy it was to share my faith with him," Art explained. "He was receptive. He listened to me and I listened to him. I thought I wouldn't be able to share my faith, but it wasn't hard at all. The experience affirmed for me that I could do this. Our job was to share, not to convert."

After their initial orientation to the region, Art and Denise went to Germany to train with people from fifty countries preparing for missionary work. Then the Smiths returned home long enough to raise all the funds for the assignment, sell their cars, and rent their home.

"We were back in Lebanon, in the field, five weeks later," Denise said.

Denise was an assistant to the field leader, whose office assigned teams to Jordan, Syria, and Iraq.

"The mission office was a temporary shelter," Denise said. "We were the connection point for email, training, distributing per diem for food and clothes, and providing local transportation."

"We were in charge of caring for the teams' personal lives," Art said, "so the volunteers could succeed in their missions. I took their cars for inspections and repairs. I repaired all the computers. Denise and I planned travel for the short-term teams and the people they would see. We hosted incoming and outgoing teams at our place, and I often drove them to their assignments."

Denise added to Art's summary.

"We managed the mission office created to render aid—food, medicine, and other supplies—to communities. We handled everything from airport pickup to receiving mail. The office had been neglected for so long, it was barely livable. We built bunk beds and provided hospitality to 400 to 500 people each year. I made connections with hundreds of people who wanted to make a difference in other people's lives."

Art and Denise belonged to a church in Beirut, but after three months living in the capital, they moved to a furnished flat in Aley owned by a Druze family from Venezuela who spoke Spanish.

"The apartment was in the basement," Denise said, "so it was always dark. We didn't have a washer or dryer, and there were no drawers in the tiny kitchen. The seating was hard as a brick, but we were given new mattresses. The landlord and his wife became great friends to us. For people harder to reach, I baked cookies and taught the children numbers and colors.

"Around us, there were a few single-family homes, but most families lived in apartments built on the mountainsides. Some women might work in a small dry goods store, but only men worked the cash registers, and only men handled the family businesses. Generally, the women cooked, cleaned, and raised the children. Of course, in Beirut, women were better educated and more a part of the workforce."

"The people were so friendly, warm, and hospitable," Art said. "When we visited someone at their home, they'd send their child to buy food, so we would stay and eat a meal with them. We became friends with local people and broke the molds they had in their minds about who Christians were. I saw people change, and I felt that what I was doing had meaning."

Reflecting further, Art added, "Most Muslims we met didn't know any Christians. Generally, people of the two faiths didn't mingle. If a job required them to talk with each other, they did, but they mostly they lived separately. I saw people change their attitude toward Americans as well as Christians. People only knew what they saw in the movies. When they got to know us, they learned we were totally different from that."

"We did our best to blend in," Denise said, "but as time went on, I realized we'd never fully understand the culture. I have the resources and education to navigate my culture, but I didn't know how to do that in Lebanon. I'd never lived abroad and didn't know what to expect. But I soon learned that people weren't wrong. They were just different from us.

"We met people of every religion and ethnicity, but we didn't discuss religion. We respected everyone, and we weren't there to create divisions or to be political. No one at Operation Mobilization tried to convert people. Our job was to help people who needed medicine, food, water. Our job was to teach and train. Why do people go on mission trips if not to help others?"

Year followed year as Art and Denise thrived in their new location, living their values and in that way honoring their deceased son, Jesse.

Peace of Thread:
Born in the USA

For the LORD your God . . . ensures that orphans and
widows receive justice. He shows love to the foreigners living
among you and gives them food and clothing. So you, too,
must show love to foreigners, for you yourselves were once
foreigners in the land of Egypt.
—Deuteronomy 10:18-19

AFTER SIX YEARS, DENISE WANTED TO COME HOME FROM LEBANON and
spend time with her grandchildren before they became teenagers. Her
parents were plagued by health problems, and her brother was eager to turn
over the care of their parents to Denise. For Art, the decision was not as clear.

"We had become friends with all the local people in Aley—our village in
Lebanon—and we were like grandparents to many young families," Art told
me. "I wanted to stay there forever and just come home once a year to visit
our family. Our children had their own lives."

But in 2011, the Smiths left Lebanon. Back in Atlanta, Art felt adrift.

"When we went to Lebanon, the trainers told us we'd have reverse culture
shock when we returned to the States, and they turned out to be right," Art
said. "Readjusting was so hard. I couldn't stand Americans, so materialistic
and indifferent to the needs of other people."

Soon, Art himself became a casualty of the American culture he lamented.
At the time, he was fifty-eight years old and unable to find a job, despite his
experience.

"I got into such a bad place, I started drinking. I prayed every day to stop. I
knew I had to overcome it, but I couldn't do it on my own. Denise was angry
because drink had ruined so many lives in her family."

Art enrolled in a local recovery program based on scripture, and he hasn't
touched alcohol since. He resumed his repair and remodeling business, lost
weight, and reversed diagnoses of diabetes and high blood pressure.

For Denise, reentry was smoother. She reconnected with friends from her
church who were teaching a two-week English class in a summer day camp
for Iraqi refugee children. The classes were held at a Clarkston apartment

Artisan Threaders

complex where many refugee families lived. Realizing that Denise had learned to speak Arabic, the friends urged her to interact with the mothers, who sat on the sidelines and watched.

"Because I could speak Arabic, I could welcome them, encourage them, answer their questions, and possibly befriend them. My ability to speak their language was key to my acceptance by the women."

While the children were attending their class, Denise spread out a large blanket on the ground where she and the Iraqi women sat together and shared stories, cookies, and tea. The women were of different religious and ethnic backgrounds, and their experiences in conflict situations had made them wary of each other.

"The women were troubled," Denise said. "They were lonely but scared. They had nothing to do and didn't know who they could trust."

Denise started to think about what the women might like to do and concluded that a shared activity might spark camaraderie. In talking with her friends, she thought of sewing. As a teenager, Denise had learned to sew, and when her daughter Danielle was in middle school, Denise became proficient at sewing by making skating costumes.

"Danielle started competitive roller skating and needed special wear made of bathing suit material, which is very hard to work with. I taught myself, figuring things out as I went."

Denise asked the women if they'd like to sew for a couple of weeks, and they said, Yes. Collaborating with her friends, Denise worked up a plan.

"The first week, the mothers learned how to use a sewing machine, and while they learned, they listened to each other's stories and became friends. We used inexpensive fabric and taught them to make a bag, no lining. We showed them how to do a corner. By the end of the second week, some women had the hang of it and some didn't, but they all liked it."

When the two-week language class for the children was over, the women were without a place to go for sewing. A friend advised Denise to introduce herself to Ahmed, the apartment manager and a refugee himself, who lived in the apartment complex with his wife, Najah. Denise told him about the women's interest in sewing, and he immediately took to the idea. He offered a basement room and helped Denise make a flyer in Arabic inviting women to a two-week sewing project. The location was perfect since interested participants could easily walk to it.

Denise then gathered a few friends, collected fabric, rounded up some old sewing machines, and sought out patterns for making sleeves for laptop computers and tablets. When she arrived back in Clarkston for her first new session, nine women came to sew, and the first stitch was made in what would become a productive workshop.

"We met in the basement for about two years," Denise said. "By the second year, we realized we were onto something, but we weren't a business yet. Then we moved to the apartment complex's community room. Next, when we couldn't find a place, we operated out of my car. We went apartment to apartment to work with the women who were sewing. After that, we were offered another community room in a complex of townhomes that Ahmed also managed."

Denise explained how the products developed.

"We started with the laptop sleeve, which had a small tab at the top," she said. "Then we added a flap and a strap. We started by putting a strap on the sleeve and figuring out how to make it into a purse. A boutique owner sat with us at a sewing table and helped us see how the bags would differ from the sleeves."

From the very start, the project demanded energy and creativity.

"The sewing machines I'd found weren't portable, they were in cabinets. The leasing company for the apartments couldn't be responsible for the equipment, so I had to tear down and set back up each sewing day. The classes lasted several hours. The refugee women never came on time, and when they showed up, they came with their children. I had one volunteer who watched the babies and another who helped me. All we had for the kids were coloring books and crayons."

It was at the townhomes that I first witnessed the workshop in action, and by the time I discovered it in 2015, the enterprise had evolved into a humming, nonprofit organization for the hand manufacture of cloth handbags and accessories.

Denise recalled for me how one milestone in the nonprofit's development had happened through word of mouth.

"I was invited to a church in northwest Atlanta," Denise said, "to speak to a group of women who were making a trip to Lebanon. As part of that visit, I told them about the work the refugee women were doing. Soon after, one woman who had been in the audience, a hairdresser, told a client about the refugees' cloth handbags. The woman was an interior designer, and she had a brainstorm."

The designer worked at the Atlanta Decorative Arts Center (ADAC) in the city's upscale Buckhead neighborhood. ADAC comprises showrooms where interior designers select high-quality products for clients. The vendors have books and books of fabric samples on hand so designers can select materials for furniture, draperies, and other design purposes. Every few months, the manufacturers change their fabrics and the vendors discard the old books to make room for the new. The designer recognized the potential of the old books.

"She called me, got passes to get me and a few volunteers in the next day, and we came home with cars filled with fabric."

Now, rather than simply allow the fabric books to be thrown away, a volunteer collects the outdated but high-end materials from ADAC and delivers mountains of fabric swatches to Denise's home. The fabric samples eventually become part of the stylish handbags.

"Motivation sure went up when I showed the women the gorgeous fabrics! We knew we'd have a better product we could sell for more money."

When I first visited, about ten refugee women were active either at home or in the workshop, although twice as many have worked simultaneously at other times. A small card, slipped inside each bag, carries the first name of the sewer, or "artisan threader," and her country of origin. Being personally associated with a creative product is a source of pride for the threader and a personal connection for the buyer.

I sat down on a stool to take in the room. Lining one wall were four tall bookcases holding fabrics sorted by color, texture, and weight. On another wall, handbag patterns, organized in see-through bags, and donated leather belts and neckties hung from hooks and rods. Below them was a ten-foot-long table piled high with fabric. Against another wall, bookcases held spools and spools of thread, bins of costume jewelry, and small pieces of leather. Against the fourth wall were tables for four sewing machines and a tiny ironing sleeve and iron for pressing seams. Below these tables, large mesh bags—labeled small, medium, and large—bulged with fabric scraps. A large worktable for cutting patterns and assembling fabric pieces filled the center of the room.

"Some of the threaders had seen a treadle machine used by a grandmother, and some had used one," Denise told me, "but most of the women had never sewn before except by hand—with a needle and thread. Some women had made clothes, but a handbag is completely different. The kinds of textiles we use aren't easy to work with, especially because of their weights. Learning to do a good job with heavy fabrics takes patience, perseverance, and an eye for detail."

The price of the product, I realized, is in the training, which Denise then told me about. Each woman's experience is different, both in terms of what she brings and how quickly she gets up to speed.

Making a Strap

"Training usually lasts four to six months, sometimes less for women who are experienced at sewing or who learn by seeing. Many of the women I've met from Afghanistan—as one example—have incredible sewing skills. Some women haven't had any formal education, and we have a lot to teach them. How fast a woman catches on also depends on whether we can speak the same language."

Refugee women tend to hear about Peace of Thread from their friends or neighbors, and Peace of Thread maintains a waiting list of women interested in being threaders. When a woman comes in to ask about training and work, she's asked to complete an application. Sometimes a husband completes the application for his wife and serves as an interpreter for training; otherwise, a woman finds someone else who knows English and then brings the application back. When a spot opens, an applicant is contacted.

Training happens at the workshop and follows a standard pattern.

"Before a woman can graduate," Denise explained, "she has to demonstrate that she can sew three bags—a small, easy one, a medium-sized one, and a hard one—without help. When she can make the bags without asking questions, she can work at home. Some women find they can't make the bags and quit the program. Maybe they're just not detailed enough or can't make a straight line. Other women sew with us for six months or nine months or two or three years or longer. Some women take some time off and come back."

One refugee woman—Ahmed's wife Najah—has been with Peace of Thread since its beginning. Now she is a trainer, a manager, and an occasional interpreter for Arabic-speaking women, and she's paid a salary. Najah designs and cuts the patterns for every new woman who enters the program, and keeps track of all the handbags used for training. Another refugee, Emain, is a former trainer who now spends her weekdays doing other work. Sometimes she comes by the workshop for a couple of hours on Fridays and volunteers to answer threaders' questions. She also helps at weekend sales events.

"That woman can sell a bag," Denise exclaimed. "She talks with the customers and she speaks on behalf of all the refugee women."

Denise herself serves as the quality control department, and she estimates she returns about fifteen percent of bags for revision or additional work. When Denise finds a problem, she either visits the threader at home or waits until the woman comes in to talk about her work. Denise believes the interaction and feedback is healthy and productive; she wants the women to succeed.

"Our communication about the work lets them know we care about them."

The day I visited, the workroom bustled with activity. One volunteer cut fabric and worked on a pattern design. Denise chose and cut fabric for several patterns. Four refugee women—Freshta from Afghanistan, Louna from Syria, and Baada and Ahdebahng from Iraq—sewed. Floor fans worked overtime, assisting a poorly functioning window air-conditioning unit.

While the women worked, visitors came and went, each one welcomed with warm hugs and sisterly kisses. Threaders who worked offsite came in to exchange work. Volunteers arrived with pinned patterns and left with fabric and supplies for other tasks. Potential volunteers came to ask how they could help. Denise was patient with questioners and worked through constant interruptions. A new volunteer, recently arrived from Los Angeles, offered her skills: she'd take photographs of the bags for the Peace of Thread website and create twenty-second clips for posting on YouTube. Later I learned that volunteer never returned, and I wondered how much of Denise's time was lost to well-meaning people whose offers never actually materialized.

Denise had a committed set of volunteers who gave time from their full lives and other commitments. Patsy was one of these volunteers. I watched while she trimmed a set of nearly completed bags. She culled the storehouse of donated jewelry, chains, fringes, jump rings, and leather, carefully selecting decorative touches that fulfilled the pattern's requirements and added to the bag's style and color. Sometimes, completed bags that don't sell during one season are reworked to make them appealing for the next season. Two volunteers reported on sales at a recent festival and the success of advertising on social media.

While the women worked, I sat with a flipchart and studied the pages, one for each product, labeled by name and dimensions and illustrated with a photo. The prices ranged from sixteen dollars for eyeglass cases to three hundred and fifty dollars for bags made from the most richly textured, expensive fabrics.

That day, the team was working on products for two upcoming arts festivals. While the Peace of Thread website has an online store, festivals, conferences, and outdoor markets account for most sales. Peace of Thread's attendance at such events is costly in terms of time, booth space, and energy to transport and set up the products, maintain the booth in hot and humid weather, and manage the sales. But the events consistently result in enough income to make the marketing approach worthwhile. A neighborhood festival, for example, might bring in more than two thousand dollars over a weekend.

When I left the workroom with Denise that day, we talked about the mission of Peace of Thread. While teaching the women to sew was primary, everyone involved in the enterprise inevitably contributes to helping the refugee women with other needs. Sometimes volunteers drive women to medical appointments; sometimes a husband needs help finding a job; sometimes hospital visits to family members are called for. To keep track of needs, Denise keeps lists of people to contact.

On a return visit to the Peace of Thread workshop, I listened to an in-depth discussion about the intricacies of product design and fabrication, the shapes and sizes of bags. Should clutch bags have embroidered material on the outside but a solid fabric on the inside that picked up an outside color? Did the pom pattern need a wider strap? Should the bobby tab be smaller? Many decisions went into the creation of standard patterns.

While sorting and hanging fabrics, Denise pointed out an area I hadn't noticed—bins labeled with each threader's name. Here the workers—both onsite and those who work from home—place finished pieces for Denise's quality review and take out new assignments along with checks for the money they earn. Every woman receives half the sales price of each bag she makes.

Denise told me about an earlier project with a church friend that had challenged the threaders. In the fall of 2014, children's book author Erin Burchik, who had volunteered with Peace of Thread since its inception, asked if the threaders could create kits for making stuffed animals to accompany her newly published Christmas book, *Animals of the Nativity*. The book's illustrator designed the animals, and Denise created the fabric patterns. Then she trained several threaders to make the kits—three hundred and eighty, which quickly sold out. Now Peace of Thread's sideline making children's book tie-ins is on hold while the author assesses her needs. When the book sales were at their peak, however, Peace of Thread's products gained exposure from the joint promotion.

Denise always looked ahead. She thought about the nonprofit's long-term health and how it could serve not only the refugee families but also the volunteers who took great satisfaction from working with Peace of Thread. She told me about a place she had found for storage and for training volunteers who didn't want to drive into Clarkston. She had established an outpost on Grace Fellowship property outside metropolitan Atlanta.

A few days later, I followed Denise's driving directions and arrived at a house with an inviting front porch and an expanse of green lawn. I parked, walked up the front steps, and slid into a rocker where I could admire the peaceful setting. The church uses the house for conferences, trainings, wedding and baby showers, and fundraisers. When Denise arrived, she led me past the house to a refurbished barn.

Artisan Threader Nuam

Inside the barn, former horse stalls were filled with fabric and decorative trim. In one stall, a large cutting table was set up and piled with yet more fabric. Near the stalls was a desk for dropping off donations to what Denise calls Peace of Thread Northeast. Here volunteers from the county northeast of the Clarkston area deliver, store, and pick up supplies and are trained in how to select fabric, pin patterns, and cut material.

The northeast location, I found out, was not Peace of Thread's only outpost. In 2013, Renee Lamb, a Mississippi resident who had crossed paths with Denise when volunteering in Lebanon, invited refugee women in her area to create a chapter of the sewing enterprise in Memphis, Tennessee (see Chapter 9).

While we were exploring the barn, Denise Flanders, Peace of Thread's lead designer since 2011, joined us. "The other Denise" guides the volunteers in their chosen assignments and troubleshoots design issues. A little later, Renee, the executive director of the Memphis chapter, came in.

When she arrived, I took stock of the three women. Denise Smith, I thought to myself, dresses like she's expecting to have fun, which I imagined was uplifting to the people around her. That day she wore flared pants, a black and white crocheted blouse trimmed with lace, a vest, black patent-leather slides, and an assemblage of jewelry—beads, earrings, and bracelets. The other Denise had her own style she calls boho chic. She wore straight jeans trimmed with lace, a blue blouse with wide sleeves, and a matching chiffon vest. Feathers fluttered in her blonde hair, tassels shook as they pleased, and her earrings and bracelets jangled. In contrast, Renee seemed conservatively dressed in knee-high boots, straight jeans, a long dark shirt, and only one necklace. Some refugee women who come to Peace of Thread wear hijab, the traditional Muslim headscarf that is a symbol of their dignity. Renee and the Denises, I noted, managed a different standard of modesty and panache, one that was entirely their own.

I listened while the leaders of Peace of Thread talked about a new design: The Lebanon Bag. They considered the type of stitching; the placement of the straps, pockets, snaps, and fringe; the weight of the fabric; the preferred color. Together they decided to create a sample bag to judge pocket placement, fringe movement, and pricing. I learned that clutch bags are as difficult to create as large bags because attention to detail is paramount. Quality finishing takes time, thought, and lengthy training. The lining can be tricky but essential to an attractive product. Denise Smith summed up her philosophy about Peace of Thread's products.

"The handbags we create are like the women. Each one is unique, and they all speak to our hearts."

By 2016, Peace of Thread had outgrown its space in the community room of the Clarkston townhomes. Having the barn for overflow storage and work was helpful, but even that site was being pushed to its limits.

Then one day, I learned from Denise that Peace of Thread had moved, and she invited me to visit the new location in Clarkston. When I pulled into the driveway, I stopped and stared at a charming, gabled house with stone pillars and a welcoming red door. I checked the address on my slip of paper and then I felt anxious. What if they couldn't make the payments? What if they had to move again?

I walked up a small set of steps and across a front porch, relishing the homey feeling. Denise's assistant, Stephanie, came out.

"Pretty nice, huh?"

I went inside, walked through a living area, and passed into another room where volunteers were at a huge cutting table with space all around it. Sturdy shelving units held the fabric and trimmings. In an adjacent room, several refugee women were sewing at machines under the watchful eyes of Emain and Najah. I continued exploring, and I found a full kitchen, a bathroom, an office, and a training area that Stephanie used when meeting with volunteers. Upstairs, I found another work area and storage for completed bags and all the equipment and supplies needed for weekend fairs. Then I tracked down Denise and asked for the whole story.

"We were browsing the web one day," Denise told me, "looking for the next place to move. We were getting an idea of price per square foot for houses renting in the Clarkston area. Surely there would be something we could afford. We needed more than one room, and I could tell our days of free space were coming to an end."

In the Internet search for rental properties, a group of small houses for sale near the original apartment complex popped up.

"We drove by to look at them," Denise said, "and one of them seemed exactly right. The women could even walk to it. There were sidewalks, and the bus came nearby. But it was out of our price range. We realized it was a dream, but we began praying about it. From time to time, we looked online to see if someone had bought it but no one had. We didn't know if our dream could become real, but we kept praying."

Months later, Denise got a call that a marketing firm in Clarkston was closing its billboard bag department, the bags companies use to advertise their name or their products. The owner of the firm had heard about Peace of

Thread and offered all the company's sewing supplies.

"I played phone tag with the owner for two weeks but finally got a text message giving me the company's address. I got into my car, plugged the address into my GPS, and when my cell phone rang, I started talking while driving. I was on autopilot, still talking on the phone when the GPS said the destination was in three hundred feet. I looked over and saw the house we had prayed about! I was stunned. Compose yourself, I told myself. Breathe. Go in and see what they have."

The realtor responsible for renting or selling the property was waiting to walk Denise through the house. Inside, Denise found shelves, sewing tables, grommet fastener supplies, a huge cutting table, and other materials handbag makers can appreciate.

"'You can have anything you want,' the realtor told me. I tried not to stop breathing," Denise said. "My dream house had nothing in it. I just liked the *outside* of the building and the location. I wanted a house in Clarkston convenient for the refugees, but this house was already laid out for Peace of Thread! It had everything we needed and more than I ever dreamed of."

Part of the house was rented to a company that was training refugees in cleaning houses and apartment buildings. The company was renting the upstairs of the house and using the detached garage to store equipment. Denise asked the realtor if the owner would allow Peace of Thread to store the supplies there until it found a place to rent or buy. The realtor gave Denise the owner's name and directed her to a house at the end of the block where he was working.

"I walked down and introduced myself to the owner. I simply told him that I needed the house. 'If I win the lottery, I'll give it to you,' he said. He needed to sell. So I asked about storing the items and he said yes."

Immediately, Denise called her friend Erin, the children's book author, who was on staff at Grace Fellowship. Denise took her to see the house, and she too immediately saw the potential. By then, Grace Fellowship dreamed of multiple supports for the refugee community—a medical clinic, counseling services, and English classes for women—in addition to a robust Peace of Thread enterprise.

"Erin said, 'We're going to get this house. We just have to put it in front of the right people,'" Denise recounted. "She said if enough people in all our circles each gave us $25, we could buy the house."

The women knew that a lot of people at Grace and in the wider community were doing good work for the Clarkston refugees, including teaching English and offering job training. Denise saw the house as a place everyone could

© Frannie Fabian

Denise Flanders, Peace of Thread Designer

come to, where the refugees could get emotional, physical, and spiritual help.

"Maybe we could share the space and share the rent," Denise thought.

She went back to the owner.

"I asked if we could rent the house for three months with an option to buy and rent some of its space to other groups working with refugees. The owner said yes."

Denise continued, explaining how the financial commitment was met.

"We wrote letters to nonprofits asking for help. Donations were funneled through Grace Fellowship, and donors could get a tax deduction. We raised $2,660 in three months through small donations from nonprofit organizations, churches, and individuals. Grace Fellowship wrote a check covering the total rental cost."

After a short interruption to brew us some coffee, Denise told me more.

"So, Grace Fellowship entered into a six-month lease with an option to buy, and the owner came down $32,000 from the original price. We needed the time to gather up enough money to buy the house. A donor writing us a check was unlikely."

In the meantime, Erin had been talking with the church's mission team, pastor, and board of directors about raising funds. Since Grace Fellowship had signed the lease on the property, Denise gave the congregation monthly updates, and the church began a fundraising campaign. To help raise awareness and funds, Peace of Thread held open house multiple times and featured guest speakers, including refugee women and representatives from refugee resettlement agencies who spoke about the need for the house.

"We wanted people from all the Grace campuses to participate so we could broaden our base of mentors," Denise explained. "We want the refugees to know we're all here to help them in every way."

To purchase the house, the seven Grace campuses, Peace of Thread, and the nonprofit organizations that would use the house needed to raise $246,000. A social media firm created a video about the artisan threaders at Peace of Thread and refugee men in The Lantern Project [now called Tekton], another Clarkston nonprofit, which trains and certifies its participants in woodworking, electrical work, plumbing, and other trades. Art teaches masonry, electrical work, and carpentry in the program. The fundraisers promoted the video through social media channels that made donating just a click of a button.

"The response exceeded our wildest expectations," Denise said. "We did it! Together, Grace Fellowship's seven campuses agreed to the purchase, and in June 2016 the property became theirs."

I sat back and breathed a sigh of relief while Denise went on.

"We met with everyone who would use the house. We talked about living together peacefully for the same mission and asked for commitment to work as a team to change lives. We emphasized the need to care for the house over the long term. A lot of people are going to come and go in this space, and a lot of time and effort will be needed to keep it in shape."

Denise went on to explain how she hoped the house would be used.

"We planned to train on Wednesdays and Fridays. We wanted to have dinners here with refugees and other groups of people so everyone would get to know each other, and they did. When dinner is served, the refugee women aren't under pressure to cook, and they have a chance to get out of the house. During dinners, the refugees learned about our culture while we learned about theirs. They shared their experiences and needs, and we found out how well they were assimilating into the community. We wanted to find different ways to help the refugees feel safe, to know they can trust us to be good neighbors. New people are moving into the Clarkston area, bringing industry and services. These newcomers need to learn about the refugee workforce."

While Denise takes great satisfaction in the successful purchase of the property, she remains focused.

"At the end of the day, we are about empowering refugees. That's really the mission of this house."

Change is constant for Peace of Thread. Just a year after moving into the house, the threaders moved out to allow room for additional projects that members of Denise's church initiated for Clarkston's refugees. Peace of Thread now occupies an outbuilding on the property that was refurbished for the sewing enterprise. The house now serves volunteers and refugees engaged in Tekton, English-language classes, psychological counseling, medical outreach, and other initiatives.

One project sprang up in a detached garage situated between the house and Peace of Thread's building. The repurposed garage now serves as headquarters for Intertwined Candles—handmade scented candles in recycled glass bottles. Like Peace of Thread, the candle-making initiative offers refugee women the chance to learn a skill and earn some income.

Erin spoke to me about the philosophy behind this cluster of activity, now known as Grace Village.

"We realized that, together, these initiatives make up a village of support that surrounds the refugee families," she said. "We want the refugees to feel loved and cared for through these various expressions of our Grace family."

In December 2016, all seven campuses of Grace Fellowship banded together to purchase the complete set of buildings that now constitute Grace Village.

I recalled Denise telling me how she had spread out a blanket on the grounds of an apartment complex in 2011, had tea with refugee women, and engaged them in learning to sew. How far the microenterprise had come from its original thread. What accounts for its ongoing success? Persistence? Dedication? Focus? Service? Faith? No one word describes the years of effort by a woman determined to be a champion for women and a catalyst for change.

Today, Denise dreams of a healing garden on the property of Grace Village, a secluded place between the outbuildings where women can take off their scarves, soak up sunlight and fresh air, and enjoy each other's company while their children play. Maybe the garden will have a swing set for the children, Denise suggests. I imagine it will, and I know I'll stop by to visit these inspiring women.

Emain:
Take Care of My Son

Thus speaketh the LORD of hosts, saying, . . . shew mercy
and compassions every man to his brother:
And oppress not the widow, nor the fatherless, the stranger,
nor the poor . . .
    —Zechariah 7:9-10

AT PEACE OF THREAD'S TRAINING ROOM, Denise introduced me to Emain.
Later, I visited her at her small, two-bedroom unit in an apartment
complex a short walk away. I was eager to hear her story and understand her
dedication to her son and to Peace of Thread.

I sat at the dining table and watched Emain in the galley kitchen beginning dinner in a way that only years of experience can perfect. She brought
two cups of steaming tea to the table and began to tell me about her life.

"I was born in a small city north of Baghdad in Iraq. My father, a military
officer, had a good education. My mother, who was born in Syria, didn't attend
school. As second cousins, they visited often and always kept in contact. My
mother was thirteen and my father was eighteen when they married. Everything is different now, people don't get married so young.

"I had eight sisters and three brothers. Two sisters passed away, one from
cancer of the blood, the other in an accident. Today one sister lives here, one
in Sweden, and one in the Emirates.[1] My three other sisters are in Iraq.

"I finished university as a civil engineer, but my certificate from Iraq
doesn't qualify me for a job in the United States. Plus, I'm fifty-six years old.
Who will hire me?

"I met my husband Luaa in 1982 at a friend's party. Luaa told this friend,
'I will choose this lady as my wife.' We talked about marrying each other,
discussed many things, and found we were in agreement. I told my father
about Luaa and that I knew when I saw him that I wanted to marry him. My
father agreed to meet with Luaa, so he came to my house.

"Soon we exchanged gold jewelry. I traveled to Baghdad to visit his
family. The groom's women must meet the bride's women, and gifts are
exchanged. We were engaged in July and married eight months later, when I

Selection of Fabrics

was twenty-one and Luaa was twenty-three. Together we worked to furnish a rented house with a salon, a dining room, a bedroom, and a kitchen. Then we prepared for the wedding party, the reception.

"I had three miscarriages before our son, Mamduah, was born. He was a special, much wanted boy, and we wanted brothers and sisters for him, but I had four more miscarriages.

"Luaa worked in the Commerce Ministry and I was in the Planning Ministry. Before graduating from college, students are tested, and those with top grades are immediately hired for jobs. Students with the highest test scores in math and chemistry go into engineering or medicine. Luaa received a high score in business subjects, so he went into commerce.

"My name was given to the Planning Ministry. I interned there for six months before my graduation and received a certificate upon completion. When I became a full-time employee, I had a week's training about the office rules. If I'd had a Master's degree, I would've started at a higher rank, but just the same, I was immediately given projects.

"My first building was a multi-tiered parking garage, and the second was a large reception complex. As time went on, I had more and more responsibility and bigger projects to supervise. Men reported to me. In Iraq, men take orders from the project engineer, whether it's a man or a woman.

"I worked on project sites, not in an office. The hours eight in the morning to three in the afternoon are considered full time. Of course, a project deadline might mean that I worked many more hours. If I had to work late, Luaa's parents, who lived with us in the early days of our marriage, took care of our son. After they died, I would let Luaa know if I would be late and he would be home for Mamduah.

"Because we were educated and had good jobs, we had a good life. After a while, we had many bedrooms in our house, and many relatives came to stay. Other families came to play cards or barbecue and stay the weekend. Sometimes, we'd stay up until early morning and then sleep late. Other times, we'd go to our relatives' houses, or we'd take a picnic and go to the lake. Our life was enjoyable, but nothing is the same now.

"In 2003, Luaa was jailed for having a satellite dish, which was banned in Iraq. Saddam Hussein didn't want people to know what was being said about him outside the country. An undercover agent, one of our neighbors, saw the dish and notified the police, who came and took Luaa away. He received a six-month sentence but served only two months.

"Every day after that, I was frightened for my husband's and my son's safety. My son's last name is Omar, which is a Sunni name. The Shia militia, supported by Iran, was targeting Sunnis. They celebrated one of their victories by killing 254 men named Omar in one week, so many on June 2, so many on June 3, and so on. It was planned. They hate my son's name just because we have an imam with that name.[2]

"My husband came home from work at four o'clock every day. But one day, at five, he still wasn't home, and I asked my son to call him. Someone from the Shia militia answered his phone. My son started screaming, 'My father has been kidnapped!' I began to shake and I heard myself screaming. The person on the line hung up. I grabbed the phone and called. The person who answered asked me, 'Sunni or Shia?' I said, 'We are all the same under God.'

"The man on the line told me the militia would free Luaa if I drove a car full of explosives to a Shia section of town. The people would see me leaving the car, and when it exploded, they could say a Sunni was responsible for killing all the people. I refused to do such a thing. I told him my husband had nothing to do with fighting, and I asked him to please release him. He hung up, and then he called the first number on Luaa's phone—his brother-in-law in Dubai—and asked him if he was Sunni or Shia and where he was. When the brother-in-law answered, the caller hung up and called the next number—Luaa's older brother—and asked the same questions. The brother swore at the caller and hung up. It was now six thirty.

"I called back and begged to talk to my husband. The kidnappers asked me, 'Why is his brother swearing at us?' and hung up. I called back. They put

Luaa on the phone. I asked him who the kidnappers were. He said, 'If I don't make it, take care of our son.' They hung up the phone. My sister called Luaa, and he told her the same thing, 'Take care of my son.' Just the week before Luaa had said, 'If anything happens, care for our son.' I laughed at the time and told him nothing would happen to us, even though we had memorized the names of the twelve Shia imams in case we were stopped and asked to prove Shia identity.

"The television news reported that American soldiers were in our area and were releasing some hostages, but they hadn't yet reached the former school where Luaa and other prisoners were being held. There were 1,075 men and women taken for interrogation. All of them were killed. I learned later that the Shia militia had blocked the road to the school to stop cars from entering there.

"At three in the morning my friend's aunt saw a man's body being thrown out of a car. She called the police, whose only job is to pick up dead bodies in the night. The police put the body in the police car, and when they stopped to get gas, the station owner, who was a neighbor, saw Luaa's body in the back seat. He said nothing because the militia was all around the station. He simply said to the police, 'Take him to the hospital. I'll tell his family.'

"It was a Saturday. All my family went to various hospitals to search for Luaa. Then my neighbor called to tell me where the police had taken his body. The driver assigned to me for my work took me to the hospital. He is Shia and my friend. When we got to the hospital, an employee asked my driver why he brought me. 'She's Sunni. You are Shia.' My driver opened my door, kissed my feet, and said not a word. What would happen if you react as a Sunni? I couldn't say a word if I wanted to live for my son.

"When I walked into the hospital, I saw bodies lying on the floor every-where. I had to step over them to get to the computer to see photos of the dead. When I saw Luaa's photo, with blood coming from his mouth, I fainted. My relatives were called to come be with me. The hospital refused to give me the body. The hospital workers said, 'Why are you picking up a Sunni body? We can get 500,000 Iraqi dinars for Sunni bodies.'[3] The militias were stuffing dead bodies with bombs and throwing them out to kill more people. One of my relatives, a professor of pharmacology, offered 750,000 dinars. They took it and we left with Luaa's body.

"We prepared his body for burial, and when we covered the body with white cloth, my son threw himself on his father and fainted. My brothers and sisters-in-law prepared the gravesite. I began forty days of mourning. After forty days, we place a headstone on the grave with the name, dates of birth

Training Center

and death, and a verse from the Qu'ran. Whatever God wishes to happen, it happens. That's what keeps us going; we believe in God.

"But we felt lost, my son and I. At forty-seven, I was a widow, afraid for my life and the life of my son. My son was devastated and shocked. He had typhus, but if I put him in a hospital, the Shia militia might kill him. I had no support from Luaa's family because they immediately left for Syria, fearing they would be next to die.

"I knew I had to get Mamduah out of Iraq because the militia had Luaa's phone with the names and numbers of all his contacts. Yet one week after Luaa died, my son had to take his national exam. I didn't expect him to pass after what he'd been through. Because I was in mourning, my sister-in-law drove my son to his school. Sick and exhausted, he went into the school and fainted, but he refused to go to the hospital until after he took the test. He didn't want to upset me.

"All our money was gone because Luaa had withdrawn all our funds the day he was kidnapped. Militias had been robbing banks, and now the kidnappers had our money too. My family stepped in to provide us support. Now I could get Mamduah out of Iraq.

"I was so scared. Mamduah was thirteen, and it was illegal for a minor to leave Iraq without his parents. A friend in airport security quietly put him on a plane to Syria where he would be safe with my nephew.

"After Mamduah was gone, I put on a long robe and gloves to disguise myself and walked to the school. My son had scored 89 out of 100. I walked the three and a half miles to my sister's, crying the whole way. I was overwhelmed by Mamduah's grade. It was our silver lining, a present from God and a gift my son gave to me and his father, and it gave me added hope to continue.

"Three months later, I locked the door of my house and left Iraq. Everything that mattered was no longer there. The first night in Syria, I slept with my son. When I tried to leave him, he said, 'No momma, don't let me go.' He hugged me all night long. He asked me over and over what we were going to do. I told him I needed to rest and think.

"We lived with family in Syria for five years, from 2008 until 2013, waiting approval of our application for asylum. We had no idea where they would send us. I applied to the United Nations for food stamps and some money to help us until we could leave.

"Finally we were approved to come to the United States. When we flew into Atlanta, a representative from New American Pathways[4] who spoke Arabic met us at the airport and took us to a two-bedroom apartment in Clarkston. The apartment had some utensils, a used sofa, and new mattresses. We had a case manager and a phone number to call if we were sick or had a problem. Someone from the agency took us to the doctor for a checkup. We were required to attend English classes, and our landlord took us to classes. We learned how to use public transportation. The agency paid our utilities and rent and the US government gave us $150 per month and food stamps for eight months. My son started working at Thriftown grocery store. A relative in North Carolina bought us a television to help us with language. We threw ourselves into studying and had little time to think about home or the past. In fact, from the moment I put my feet on the ground, I started studying English. After ten days in the country, I asked about my son's studies. He needed one more semester of high school, which he finished.

"One day when Mamduah was working at the grocery store, some men came to shop. They asked him why he wasn't in college. He explained that he had been here only three months. One man said, 'You must be in college. Your face shows you are from a good family.' Even though he didn't know my son, he helped him pay for an admissions test. The man was an American who worked in financial aid at Georgia Perimeter College. Mamduah was so happy, and he asked me, 'How can I repay this person?' But I know when God took his father—or any person's father—God will be the father of the boy. Six months after arriving in America, Mamduah started college.

"I met Denise in September 2013, three months after our arrival. A friend told me about her sewing near my apartment. I walked in to see what she was doing, and then I started going every Wednesday and Friday to learn how to design and cut. Denise was the first American I met. She introduced me to American ways. Now she is like my sister. I was a stranger, and I needed someone to say, 'How are you? How are you doing?'

"In July 2014, the stress of all that had happened to me caused a heart attack. I wasn't feeling well, and after several days, a friend took me to the hospital. I didn't know I had had a heart attack, and I'm grateful that I recovered. Denise visited me and organized people to stay with me for tests and help me get paperwork straightened out. Then *she* had to be hospitalized with a kidney infection! Denise and Art did so much to help us during that scary time.

"Our apartment manager told the manager of a local college about me and that I have a good character. As a refugee, you have to learn the language, the culture, how to treat people, and what they like. The college wants people to be satisfied with its programs. Now I work for the college as a telemarketer, eight hours a day, four days a week, for ten dollars per hour.

"On Fridays I work for Denise. Depending on sales, some months I earn nothing, some months $400 or less. Denise has three of my bags for two big sales, and I'm sewing more and more. Festivals are coming up. I get fifty percent of sales of my bags.

"Last year, my employer nominated me for the Best Refugee in Atlanta award because I help people and have done so well in English. For this honor, I was interviewed by local television. When I was on the air, I thanked President Obama for greeting Muslims during Ramadan. I greeted my family, and then I talked about Peace of Thread.

"In October 2016, we moved from the apartment to our first house in America with help from my family. We chose one most like our house in Iraq. My son has graduated from junior college and is starting university. He also has a full-time job with a construction company. He too helps me pay the bills.

"Denise wants to educate Americans about Iraqis, and she has asked me to speak to people at her church and elsewhere. Many people seem surprised that we are educated. Some people think we are still walking with camels and have no culture. I would like Americans to know that we had a good life in Iraq. We built our house and paid for it. When we went to the hospital and got medicine, there was a small copay, about one dollar. If you were in a car accident, you paid out of pocket instead of paying for car insurance. We didn't pay property tax or sales tax, no taxes of any kind. My salary was $1,000 per month and my husband's was too. Education was free, there was food for the poor, and even rents were low. It was a good life."

Denise's Circles:
Comfort, Care, & Commitment

At the end of every third year, bring the entire tithe of that year's harvest and store it in the nearest town. Give it to the Levites, who will receive no allotment of land among you, as well as to the foreigners living among you, the orphans, and the widows in your towns, so they can eat and be satisfied. Then the LORD your God will bless you in all your work.
—Deuteronomy 14:28-29

DURING MY VISITS TO THE PEACE OF THREAD WORKSHOP, I watched and listened. Sometimes, conversation was minimal as the women concentrated on designing, measuring, cutting, and sewing. I heard only the scratch of pencils, the snip of scissors, and the hum of sewing machines. But most often, chatter broke out in several languages, and the front door seemed to revolve as the threaders who worked from home and visitors came and went. When I tried to talk with Denise, I learned that no conversation with her ever went uninterrupted.

Over time, I came to see Denise as a center of many orbits. Staff, volunteers, threaders, and other refugees—family and friends—are like planets that move in the aura of grace, compassion, determination, and optimism Denise projects. She has a dedicated following of women who try never to let her down because of their profound appreciation. Mutual love and respect are the forces that keep the multiple orbits in motion.

One woman, Stephanie, occupies a vital place in this universe of threaders. As Peace of Thread's operations manager, Stephanie shoulders responsibilities for Denise and the refugee women. Stephanie is Denise's right hand, but their relationship goes far beyond the professional. Stephanie shared with me how she and Denise came to know each other and what Denise means to her.

"I got to know Denise in 2002," Stephanie said, "when some of us from Grace Fellowship went on a mission trip to Orlando. As team leader, Denise drove down ahead of us. When I got off the bus, Denise was standing there, and her first words to me were, 'Your shorts are too short.'"

Denise's comment had surprised Stephanie, but it was a reprimand she never forgot.

Time for a Party

The next year, Stephanie was in college when her mother died of cancer and her father started drinking in an attempt to diminish his sorrow. Stephanie took a more healthful way to cope with her grief.

"I joined a discipleship group at Grace Fellowship for women in their late teens and early twenties, all of whom had lost a parent," Stephanie said. "My brothers are much older than I am, and they were long gone from the house."

Denise learned of Stephanie's loss and her troubled living situation, and she invited Stephanie to move into her house.

"I procrastinated," Stephanie said. "I was afraid to leave my father because he couldn't think straight. But we didn't talk to each other, and we were losing the house because of my mother's unpaid medical bills."

The discipleship group saw that Stephanie couldn't keep living under the circumstances she described and made the decision for her.

"They showed up at my house, boxed up my bedroom, and took me to Denise's," Stephanie said. "When we got there, I found one girl painting my new bedroom. Denise had bought me a new mattress. She took me for a manicure, pedicure, and beauty makeover. I lived there until 2004, when I made a fresh start at Berry College. Art and Denise became my family."

Around the same time, Buddy, the Grace pastor, had started a course called Love Your Enemies, and Stephanie attended it. In the summer, before going back to college, she joined a mission trip Buddy led to London for people who wanted to learn from experts about Islam.

"It was my first experience with another faith and another culture," Stephanie told me.

As Stephanie's world began to expand, however, she met with another loss.

"My father had moved in with one of my brothers, but he didn't stop drinking," she said. "He could no longer drive, so he took a taxi to do his errands. Ten days after I graduated from Berry, my father was out doing errands when a driver crossed the double line of oncoming traffic and hit the taxi head on, killing the taxi driver and my dad."

To help her deal with this loss, Stephanie had a support system in place.

"I shared my grief at church Bible study. My friends' parents were like another set of parents to me, so I didn't have to struggle alone."

By this time, Art and Denise were out of the country.

"I stayed in touch with Denise and Art by phone and email. I wanted to go to Lebanon to see them but couldn't afford to. Denise came home for a short break, and she steered me to a job with an insurance company, where I started working in 2009. When Art and Denise returned and moved back into their house a couple of years later, their basement apartment became available, and I moved in. Whenever I had spare time, I helped Denise with the refugee women. I came to love them. They stirred my heart for all Muslims and for the Middle East."

In 2013 and 2014, Stephanie went to Jordan to work with Syrian refugees.

"Both times, I didn't want to leave Jordan, and I cried all the way to the airport. Then in January 2015, I was laid off from work. I felt badly for all of five seconds—until I realized I could work with Peace of Thread full time."

Before long, Stephanie became integral to the organization and essential to Denise by offering professional skills as well as the intangibles of encouragement and support.

"I do payroll. I train volunteers. I meet with potential donors, and I have home meetings with the threaders," Stephanie said. "I pick up and deliver work, and I handle logistics for our weekend events, where I tell the Peace of Thread story. I seek ways to make the work go more smoothly and quickly. I jump in wherever I'm needed."

Over time, I witnessed Stephanie taking on many roles, and I recognized that her commitment to Peace of Thread goes well beyond that of a typical employee.

"Denise has been a mother to me for the last fifteen years," Stephanie said. "Her love for me has taught me how to love others. Denise has built deep relationships with the refugee women. My reward is to give these women a voice, to empower them, to help them leave trauma behind and succeed in their new home. The women trust Denise and they confide in her because they see she is helping them have a better life. I've given her and these women my servant heart."

I thought about the feelings for Denise that Stephanie had shared with me. In addition to having her own biological daughter, Denise has a chosen daughter, and Stephanie has a chosen mother. I knew from my own experience, however, that being a mother or a mentor sometimes means showing tough love. I wondered how tough Denise could be, and I soon found out.

During my visits to Peace of Thread, I found that Denise was quick to praise good work, but when a threader came in with unfinished or poorly stitched bags, Denise let her know she was unhappy.

One day, Denise was showing me the design of a new handbag when one of the refugee threaders—I'll call her Lisha from Iraq—unexpectedly came into the workshop. She was carrying several finished bags, and she shyly handed them to Denise for inspection.

When Denise examined them, she shook her head no and showed Lisha the improper finishing. Lisha's shoulders drooped. Denise told her how unhappy she was with the work and with Lisha because she never calls to say when she's coming, if she'll be late, or if she won't be coming at all after she's made an appointment. Lisha began scooping the bags back into her satchel and started explaining about her children, a story I could tell Denise had heard many times before. Then Denise hugged her.

"I love you," she said to Lisha. "Being on time or calling is part of being responsible. Next time, will you call me?"

Lisha nodded yes and headed out the door.

After she left, I asked Denise what the problem was with Lisha's children.

"Lisha works in a bakery from five in the morning until three in the afternoon. When she gets home, she cooks, cleans, and cares for the children."

"What does her husband do?" I asked.

Denise explained that he had hurt his back at work and was now disabled, either temporarily or permanently. The doctors weren't sure as yet. I asked whether he helped with the children.

"It isn't his job to do women's work," Denise said. "Right now, it's very tough. I've been trying to find him a job where his current condition won't matter, but so far, I haven't found one. Before long, Lisha will quit her job because of the children and both of them will be unemployed."

I asked Denise why Lisha didn't understand that without her paycheck, life would be even more dismal.

"I don't know," Denise said. "She's used to having family support when there's an emergency, but there's no family here. I understand her frustration, but I couldn't take the bags. Part of being in *our* culture is to call ahead and follow through."

At the end of the workday, while I helped Denise load supplies into her car, I asked what could be done to help Lisha.

"These women have been through so much," Denise explained. "Many of them have PTSD [post-traumatic stress disorder]. In 2005, Lisha's husband was kidnapped by a militia. The family gathered all the money they had to pay the ransom. A few weeks later, the militia came back for more. She and her husband were lucky to escape with their lives."

Denise paused, then told me more.

"Lisha's from a village," Denise said. "She didn't have the benefit of an education, and she knows only the role her culture gave her. Her husband's role is to support the family, so both of them feel a loss of face. I want her to improve her sewing skills so she can stay home and still earn money for the rent and bills. I've asked family services to assess their situation and help them temporarily.[1] Tomorrow, I'll stop by their apartment to visit and take them some food."

I thought about Lisha's situation and wondered what I would do if I were dropped into a country where I didn't speak the language, had no money, and understood only the rules of a different culture. I had a glimpse into the complex situations Denise navigates on the refugees' behalf.

Another day, my visit to Peace of Thread was about design. As I came through the door, I saw Denise Flanders, the lead designer, culling through a massive stack of material. I watched as she pulled out three or four pieces of fabric, set them on the cutting table, and assessed them until she was satisfied with her choices.

I asked her how she selected the fabrics.

"I went to school for fashion and design at Perimeter College," Denise said. "I use my creative eye, which makes me feel alive. My job is to pick out fabrics, put them together, and help others do the same. I teach the refugee women and the other volunteers."

Denise has volunteered with Peace of Thread since its earliest days, working four days a week, even though she herself doesn't sew.

"Now I have a machine," she said. "I'm learning."

Denise also works in sales, at the fairs and festivals where Peace of Thread has reserved a booth. The lack of child care and transportation prevents many refugee women from participating.

Enjoying Good Conversation

"Working these events is a big commitment," Denise explained. "It takes two hours to set up, so we have to be there well before the show starts. Set up is physically tiring. All the merchandise has to be hauled in and out. There are miserable days—hot and rainy, with little traffic and few sales. Then there are times when the crowds are huge and we earn money from the sales to pay the women. Of course, if they could come to the shows, they'd be able to promote their own work, which would make it worthwhile for them."

Despite Denise's heavy time commitment to the nonprofit, some of the threaders were disturbed by her unpredictable attendance.

"Sometimes when I was very busy, I didn't make it to the workshop until three in the afternoon," Denise told me. "One of the women said to me, 'So you're finally showing up? Why don't you come earlier so I have more bags to sew?' Another time, one of them said, 'I like the way you design. Why aren't you helping me more?' Many of the women didn't understand that I'm a volunteer and that I have a life beyond here. I explain the best I can, but sometimes it takes a while for them to hear me."

That afternoon, more and more refugee women began to arrive, and Denise couldn't talk with me any longer because it would interrupt her teaching. A few days later, the two of us got together for coffee, and she told me her story.

"I met Denise Smith in 1996 at my first ever women's retreat," she said. "I was a new Christian, attending a Methodist church."

At the retreat, Denise heard women talking about Jesse, the Smiths' son, who had been ill for about three years at the time.

"I didn't know Jesse, but I got to know many people who did," Denise said. "The Grace pastor's wife, Jody, said she was giving blood because Jesse needed a transfusion. I was surprised that she would do that for a church member's child. That kind of caring was a new experience for me. I also saw how strong Denise [Smith] was."

In 2000, Denise Flanders's mother died. Her ongoing grief and the warmth she had felt from the women from Grace Fellowship prompted her to start attending Grace the following year.

"The first month I did nothing but cry. The other Denise was in charge of hospitality, and she was always kind and pleasant to me," she said. "I helped at events for the middle and high school kids, and because Denise was part of the youth ministry, we talked. She told me stories about Jesse all the time. Denise is a busy person. She's always going, and I sensed her exhaustion. But she found time to talk with me, and I felt that God was bringing us together."

When Denise and Art were in Lebanon, the two women stayed in touch as prayer partners. After Denise Smith returned and started sewing with refugee women, she told Denise Flanders about her idea of designing handbags.

"I don't sew, I don't speak Arabic, and I'd never met a person who was Muslim," Denise said. "I told Denise I'd provide buttons and other finishing touches. One day, we were at a store, and I bought some buttons for little square bags. Then she challenged me."

Denise Smith invited her friend to go with her to Clarkston to visit some women and children.

"I lived only one exit away from Clarkston, but I was terrified," Denise admitted. "I'd never been with people of the Muslim faith. What was odd, however, was that I'd just told my pastor that I'd go on a mission trip to the Middle East."

Denise's experience in Clarkston was a good orientation for that trip.

"When we arrived at the apartment, I stood in the foyer because there were so many people and they all sounded like they were yelling," Denise said. "I'd never been with a covered woman [wearing hijab]. I didn't know what they were saying. Denise told me to take my shoes off and come sit on the floor. I fell in love with every one of the women right away, and I whispered, 'God, this is quite the adventure. What are we doing here?'"

Denise Flanders expanded her commitment to Peace of Thread by joining Denise during the years she ran the project from her car.

"Back then, Denise would call the women," she explained. "We'd go to an apartment, haul in all the supplies, then sit on the floor with a couple of threaders and instruct them about the fabric. Then we'd eat, put all the supplies back in the car, and drive home. It was arduous, but that was how we built relationships."

For the Denises, even working from their cars—convertibles at the time—didn't mean doing a drive-through, as Denise Flanders put it.

"We never just hand something out the window to the refugees," she said. "We get to know the women, which takes time, lots of time. At first, I didn't understand that, and I couldn't understand why the women would want to know me.

"Once, I was in the car with one of the threaders," Denise continued, "and I said, 'A year ago you were in a different country, and I'd never have known you. Did you ever think we'd be friends driving through Clarkston? When did I wake up and decide to know someone from Baghdad?' Now I see how we're interconnected.

"I was divorced in 2013, which was traumatic for me. But my ordeal was trivial compared with what the refugees have been through. By working with the refugee women, I've learned about different cultures, about suffering and sacrifice, and about hospitality. I've expanded my ability to love and become friends with people who are different from me, who don't speak my language. We can speak a universal language by laughing and smiling. Getting to know the refugee women has increased my compassion."

In 2017, Denise remarried, and she and her husband now live in a small community near Athens, Georgia. The trip to Clarkston takes time, so she's considering working from home or opening another chapter of Peace of Thread near her.

"I've learned a lot about myself and my creativity," Denise said. "Close to a thousand bags have my stamp incorporated into them."

During my next visit to Peace of Thread, I saw refugee women sewing at machines, learning to measure, identifying bag shapes, choosing thread colors, or putting fabrics of the same weights in order on the shelves. Volunteers were helping with pinning and cutting patterns. In all their work, the women used fabrics Denise Flanders had selected.

Another day, Denise Smith promised me time without interruptions, and I went to her home planning to ask all the questions about Peace of Thread I'd been saving up. I had barely seated myself at her kitchen table when her cell phone rang.

"Don't answer it," I pleaded, "please don't answer it."

Denise saw who was calling and said she had to answer. I sighed in defeat. Her next words to me were, "Come on, we have to go. We can talk in the car."

As we drove to the apartment of Sapidah, a woman from Afghanistan, and her family, Denise told me the backstory.

"Sunday was Father's Day, and I was with Art and my family when Sapidah called," Denise said. "She told me she'd been in a car accident and asked if I could come. She couldn't explain to me in English where she was, so I called Kim, a volunteer in her area who speaks her language. I asked Kim to call Sapidah, go to her, and take photos of the accident. When the policeman came, Sapidah refused to speak to him because she thought he would take her to prison. Kim got it straightened out, but now a police officer is coming to Sapidah's apartment at my request. Kim and I can explain what the family is saying, and the officer can reassure them that Sapidah isn't going to jail. They're all frightened to death."

Soon after Sapidah arrived from Afghanistan, a volunteer from World Relief, one of the resettlement agencies, brought her to Peace of Thread. At the time, she spoke no English. She's sewn with the nonprofit for three years now, and she often helps at the weekend events.

Sapidah is one of five young women, aged twenty to twenty-seven years, who live with their father and mother in a small two-bedroom apartment in Clarkston. As girls, none of the sisters had any education because their father kept them inside the house to protect them. He feared that girls would be kidnapped or simply disappear; he thought it was dangerous for any of the sisters to go out.

When Denise and I arrived at the apartment, Sapidah welcomed us in. The furnishings were minimal—two small white sofas, pale gold floor pallets with pillows, a floor fan, and a small coffee table. Curtains hung in the doorway to the kitchen.

Not long after we settled in, a police officer arrived. He was a young man, patient and polite. Denise thanked him for coming and explained to Sapidah and one of her sisters that a police officer's job is to keep us safe.

Stephanie Marbut, Director of Operations

"You mustn't be afraid when you see police," Denise told them. "You must learn to speak English so you can explain to the police what has happened. Then you can help your whole family."

At the scene of the accident on Sunday, Kim had asked the other driver for his insurance information, but he had refused to give it to her. The police officer explained that he couldn't give the information to Sapidah because of privacy laws, but he had submitted his report, and now both drivers could go to the police station and get a copy of it for five dollars.

The officer explained to everyone that when Sapidah had turned into a gas station parking lot on Sunday, she hadn't allowed enough room for the other car and had damaged it. She was guilty of the offense, but if she wanted to contest the citation, she could go to court and explain what happened.

Hearing the word "court," Sapidah's head snapped up. This was a word Sapidah knew well, and to her, the word was synonymous with jail. She said, "Jail! No!"

Denise assured her that going to court didn't mean going to jail. Then Denise thanked the policeman, showing Sapidah that she wasn't afraid of him. After he left, Sapidah's father and another one of her sisters came into the room. That day, I saw Denise respond to the needs of frightened refugees with patience, kindness, and reassurance, providing a reliable, fixed point in a realm of uncertainty.

A few days after the visit to Sapidah's apartment, I went to Peace of Thread planning to meet with another refugee. Instead, I met one of Denise's newest volunteers, April. At first, I found her reluctant to talk about herself. Instead, when children came in with their mothers, she took them outside to play while their mothers sewed. Over time, I learned about her beliefs and her journey.

April was born in Eureka, California, surrounded by redwoods and fog; by the time she was ten, she was living with her family inland, in Redding. April's career choices went from veterinarian to doctor of medicine and then settled on nursing. While volunteering at a hospital as part of her training, she realized she wanted to help heal emotions and the world's social injustices. She graduated from California State Polytechnic University with a degree in sociology and social work in 2013. In college, April had joined Cru [Campus Crusade for Christ] and led Bible classes.[2]

"After graduation I joined World Race," April told me. "I went with a group of forty young adults to partner with local long-term missionaries in eleven designated countries in eleven months. I left in January 2014 and returned on Thanksgiving Day. My group traveled to Guatemala, Honduras,

Nicaragua, Costa Rica, Thailand, Laos, Cambodia, Malaysia, the Philippines, South Africa, and Swaziland.

"In September 2015, I moved to Gainesville, Georgia, to intern with Adventures in Missions, the organization that sponsors World Race. I had no family or friends in Georgia aside from the people working at Adventures and a small group of World Race alumni. I also interned at the corporate office, first in the women's ministry department and then in the long-term missions department. I went into that internship thinking I would stay with Adventures. Instead, I began to recognize goals that went beyond the scope of the organization. I wanted to work with refugees either overseas or in the States. I wanted to be a source of hope and encouragement, especially for women who had been oppressed. A couple of months before my internship ended, I found out about Peace of Thread. I moved to Atlanta, was hired as a nanny, and began volunteering with Peace of Thread."

In August 2017, April became a staff member at Peace of Thread. As the Team Relations and Support Specialist, she coordinates volunteers, takes on special projects to help with organizational structure, and contributes to day-to-day operations. April and Stephanie now share the basement apartment in Denise's and Art's home.

"Sometimes I'm asked why I chose this work instead of going after what people think they're entitled to, living in America," April said. "For me, it's not giving up because it was never mine to begin with. I have a bed, food, a roof over my head, a car, and more clothes than I need. These things make me richer than most people on the planet. My life may not look like much, but I'm satisfied. If I were to choose money, my soul would slowly die because it would never be enough."

What is enough for April is being with the refugee women.

"I get to be a part of the lives of some amazing women from different countries," she said. "They've been through some of the worst atrocities one could think of, and they still choose to live in this world and fight for themselves and their families. I can't begin to describe how humbled I am that they allow me to be a part of their lives."

During each of my visits to Peace of Thread, I met new threaders and volunteers. One volunteer, Patsy, has been with Denise from nearly the very beginning. Today, everyone refers to Patsy as "the bling lady" because she adds the finishing touches to bags that need embellishment. Patsy comes in two days a week, and when I first met her, she was searching through tiny drawers in a cabinet filled with broken jewelry. She took time and enormous care to make the perfect choice. Like the two Denises, Patsy understands what creates an appealing product: proportion, balance, unity, and emphasis. She creates jewelry herself and has a workshop in her home. She readily embraces Peace of Thread's design goal: to create a harmonious whole and eliminate fabric or trim distractions.

Patsy was born in Vancouver, Washington. She told me that her father, a welder in the Navy shipyard, had a nervous breakdown and left the military. Her family moved to Punta Gorda, Florida, where they owned a small gas station and convenience store. From there, they moved to Miami, where her mother worked as a medical secretary. In 1954, when Patsy was ten, her father had a second breakdown, and he didn't recover. When Patsy was old enough to drive, she often went to see him at the mental health facility where he lived, while her mother worked. Before then, she and her mother went together.

At sixteen, Patsy started working at a five and dime store. At eighteen, she used her savings of $300 to buy her first car. That year she became pregnant, and she traveled to Jacksonville, Florida, to a home for unwed mothers. She gave birth to a daughter, and following an agreed upon plan, she left her baby there for adoption. Back in Miami, Patsy dreamed that God told her to go back and get her child. She did, and she and her mother began to raise her daughter together. Patsy's mother continued to work as a medical secretary, and Patsy worked as a waitress and bartender.

When her daughter was two years old, Patsy married her daughter's father. It was a mistake, and the marriage lasted only six months. Patsy said she had started living a fast and reckless life, doing drugs and selling them. After ten years, at age thirty-seven, she was reported to the police and arrested, with the prospect of a sixty-year prison sentence.

Frightened and remorseful, Patsy cried far into the night, telling God that if He would get her out of the mess she'd created, she'd become a good person. Friends and family wrote to the judge assigned to her case, explaining that she was good but gullible, that it was her first offense, and that she'd never been in trouble before. Patsy said that because of those references, her contrition, and her promise never to be in trouble again, she was sentenced to two years of probation.

A couple of years later, Patsy met her current husband, Earl, and after they married, they agreed that leaving Miami would do them both good.[3] He accepted a job transfer to Connecticut, where he continued as a field manager for a communications company and Patsy worked as a waitress. One evening a couple came in for dinner, and before eating, they said a blessing over their food. Patsy took that in and said to herself, "I want to be like them."

The residents in her town were mostly Catholic, and the only Protestant church within three hundred miles was Baptist. Earl joined that church, but Patsy worked on Sundays and wasn't able to go with him. Patsy said that women at the church prayed she'd lose her job so she could go to church with her husband. Lose it she did, and from then on, she managed the church's childcare.

About ten years after moving north, Earl was transferred to Georgia, where he and Patsy have lived for twenty-three years, attending a Baptist church in Lilburn. Patsy's pastor, who is friends with Denise and knew Jesse, invited Denise to his church on a Wednesday night to talk about Peace of Thread and show the handbags. Denise brought a few refugee women with her. Patsy loved Denise's story and decided she wanted to help. A few months later, in May 2012, Patsy retired from her job as a preschool teacher at the church. She contacted Denise to order a purse, and then started to volunteer.

After volunteering for about two years, Patsy knew about Peace of Thread's and the refugees' needs. One day she learned that a local retail store was discarding clothing, belts, and broken jewelry. Patsy picked up the unwanted merchandise, repaired everything she could, and made it all available to the refugee women. She continues this practice today. Denise says that Patsy's ability to see beauty in brokenness is an asset to Peace of Thread. She enables the nonprofit to accept more donations for the women than they otherwise could.

"The refugee women are so appreciative," Patsy said. "I love the days I work at Peace of Thread. It's brought out the artist in me, and it allows me to give to others. Denise made space and set up a table just for me."

Patsy also appreciates the benefits of Peace of Thread to the refugee women.

"Denise has a big heart for these women. She sees them when they have a baby, when they're in the hospital, or whenever they need anything. She's self-less. Stephanie and April are dedicated too. April does a good job of design. Stephanie is always there to answer questions and lend a hand. The volunteers are friendly and committed. Peace of Thread has made my life full."

I thought about the women I'd met at Peace of Thread, noticing that many of them seemed to have something in common. Whether they were from a foreign country or from the United States, in many ways nearly all the women were refugees—women who had experienced substantial loss or trauma and were seeking a place of safety. The women came from Iraq and Congo, California and Washington State, Afghanistan and Somalia, Florida and Ohio.

In some cases, the women had been the victims of political unrest; in other cases, they were the victims of poor choices stemming from inexperience or unhealthy environments. These women also shared profound faith, regardless of their religion, and steadfast hope for the future. They surrounded themselves with a positive spirit, and they embraced hard work. In all cases, they shared in the world of Denise Smith.

Collected here are the words of some of Peace of Thread's most dedicated volunteers.

Dorothy Fonde Wertz: "As a retired teacher of English to speakers of other languages and a lifelong sewer, I have found many ways to use my experience to support the work of Peace of Thread. At the training center, I help design, and I evaluate the sewing machines that need repair. I've come to know many of the threaders. Some of them come to the weekly English classes I teach in Clarkston. I spread the word about Peace of Thread's empowerment plan, and I help recruit volunteers to work as designers. I plan to continue my commitment."

Andrea Carroll: "I met the refugee women at an event at church. I was attracted to the booth by the beautiful handbags, but I fell in love with the ministry and the women. I volunteer as a 'runner' who picks up fabrics at ADAC and brings them to the workshop. I've also volunteered at a few festivals. The Lord has really blessed me by introducing me to the creativity of this ministry. I've ventured out of my community and the comfort zone of my culture. He has woven friendships and connections that I didn't expect. When I'm carrying one of my cloth handbags, someone always asks, 'Where did you get that purse?' Then I share the story of Peace of Thread."

Erin Burchik: "As a wife and mother of four children, and the author of five children's books, I have a special place in my heart for refugee women and children. After Brian and I married, we moved into an apartment complex where many refugees were housed. Our Iraqi neighbors became dear friends. From that point on, I knew I wanted to serve the refugee community. Grace Fellowship has a heart for refugees and foster families. I received enormous support from the church community that got my family through the transition of adopting our three youngest children at once. Everyone helped me with meals, prayers, and babysitting. My writing was birthed from my work in the refugee community, so my commitment feels very integrated to me."

Mary Lynn "Bitsy" Pitts: "I majored in visual design at Auburn University and had a career in advertising. I started volunteering a year ago, after holding babies while their mothers learned English at the Clarkston Community Center. A friend who taught sewing to refugee women in Clarkston told me about Peace of Thread, and I agreed it was right for me. All design isn't the same, and I've had quite a learning curve. There's more to do than choose fabrics, and as a designer, I can contribute. I've never been associated with a more loving and empowering group of women. Denise gives all the women and children who come through the door a smile and a hug, and she shows sincere concern for their welfare. When the threaders leave with their new work, they're sent off with a hug and a wish for goodness. When a purse isn't sewn correctly, Denise patiently explains the problem and how to correct it."

Barbara Johnson: "I met Denise at a Thanksgiving feast at the church after she returned from Lebanon. When she learned I could sew, she took me with her to Clarkston. I helped load, unload, and reload sewing machines and supplies. I was there with the mothers at the original church camp, inviting them to participate in the two-week sewing project. To see what has come from that experience is heartwarming. Denise has the powers of perseverance and persuasion."

Hannah Meltzer: "I met Stephanie and April at a park festival. Peace of Thread intrigued me. I was looking for a job, and I wondered if they were hiring. But helping others is something I'm passionate about. They told me about the volunteer program on Wednesdays and Fridays. I went to Grace Village and met Denise. She was so excited about having me join, I started volunteering that week and met other volunteers and refugees. I learned how to cut and design the key fob patterns and Christmas stockings. I'm starting a new job now, but I'll continue contributing to this wonderful brand."

Melanie Russell: "I'm a retired pediatric oncology social worker from St. Jude Children's Research Hospital in Memphis. I read a newspaper article in 2014 about Renee starting a chapter here. It caught my eye because it's here at First Baptist Church, where I went to Sunday school and was married. My mother was an expert seamstress and taught me to sew. I kept the article in mind, and when I was approaching retirement, I contacted Renee. I enjoy designing the purses and working with the women and helping them improve their sewing skills. I can see my mother and father's graves from the window of this training center. This project is another way for me to stay connected with my family."

Patsy Roberts, Long-Term Volunteer

Fahima:
I Learned to Drive

And He came and preached peace to you who were afar off
and to those who were near . . . For through Him we both
have access by one Spirit to the Father.
Now, therefore, you are no longer strangers and foreigners,
but fellow citizens with the saints and members of the
household of God . . .
—Ephesians 2:17-19

I FIRST MET FAHIMA, a woman from Afghanistan, at Peace of Thread. She
told me she and her family had to move from Clarkston because the renters
in the apartment below theirs constantly complained about the footsteps
overhead. It would seem a challenge to silence the steps of four children—
boys aged eleven, nine, and three years, and a girl seven years old. When I
visited the family for the first time at their new apartment two years later,
I expected a rambunctious troop. Instead, Fahima's youngest boy played
quietly at her feet while we talked, and her other children sat with us on the
living room sofas, engrossed in our conversation. That day, Fahima's husband,
Mohammad, was home, and because he speaks English well, he offered to
interpret for Fahima if needed.

Utilities are not included in the rent for Fahima's and Mohammad's
two-bedroom apartment, so they pay for electricity themselves. To save
money, the air conditioner was off despite a soaring temperature outside.
Two Afghan carpets covered the living room floor, and a weaving of Ahmad
Massoud hung near the window. Massoud, known as the Lion of Panjshir,
was an Afghan rebel who fought against Soviet forces and the Taliban; he was
killed in 2001.[1]

I looked at Fahima's round, cherubic face. Her bright eyes and heart-melting
smile drew me in as she began her story. From time to time, Mohammad
contributed.

"We lived in Kabul, Afghanistan," Fahima said. "In 2004, my husband
started working with the American military in the field as an interpreter.[2]
His life was in danger every day because of the war. The Americans said if

he worked for them for two years, we could go to the United States.[3] The American forces knew we would be killed after they left. We applied for a visa in 2008, and we finally came to the United States in 2012. Today fighting still goes on and on.

"My father was a mechanic. He and his brother were killed in 1993 when a rocket fired during the civil war hit our house.[4] I was a child at the time, and I wasn't hurt, but other members of my family were injured. I have four brothers and four sisters; one brother was only three months old when my father died. My mother had finished high school and two years of college, and was considered a well-educated woman. After my father died, she supported us alone until my oldest sister got a teaching degree and one of my brothers got a job.

"My mother was always strong and independent, and she raised us to be the same. We never asked for help from anyone but God. My brothers went to the mosque to pray, and we women prayed at home. The only advice my mother ever gave me about marriage was to be patient. Go into the bathroom and cry your eyes out, she told me, but come out smiling. She said never let anyone know when you're upset.

"My family had two homes, one in Kabul [the capital] and the other in the mountains of the Panjshir [River Valley]. Afghan fighters kept Panjshir safe because of its riches: gemstones—like lapis lazuli, emeralds, rubies, and many fruits—like mulberries. The area is safer than some places because you can see people coming from many miles away.

"The Taliban came to Afghanistan in 1996 and stayed for five years. They took away music, television, and even kites. During that time, women and girls couldn't go outside the house without a male companion, and when we went outside, we had to wear a burqa.[5] Before the Taliban came, my mother had worked as a certified first-grade teacher. After the Taliban, women could only cook and clean. If our wrists or ankles showed when we went outside, the Taliban beat us with sticks. In the villages where people have no power, this continues.

"We were so young when we married. I was eighteen, and Mohammad was twenty-one. Ours was an arranged marriage, like almost every marriage in our country. Mohammad is my cousin, and marriage between cousins is typical. Our wedding was a huge celebration—seven hundred people, all family and friends. We danced and talked until three in the morning. The imam came to the wedding hall. Like most brides, I wore green, but after the imam pronounced us man and wife, I changed to a white dress. Our wedding was so expensive that if Mohammad had paid for it himself, he would have had to save for three years, but his entire family helped.

"After the wedding celebration, I moved to my father-in-law's house and began caring for his family. This is the custom. We have no honeymoon. Mohammad has three sisters and one brother, and two uncles also lived in the family home. The house had three bedrooms and a salon, and the kitchen was in a separate building. For meals, we place a long cloth on the floor and set it with plates, tea glasses, utensils, and pots of food. We eat with our hands, but children eat with a spoon. We had our first child when I was twenty.

"Because the civil war had damaged the economy, there was no work in Kabul, and one of my brothers left for Pakistan around 1991. At that time, Afghans freely moved to Iran or Pakistan because no visa was required and it was easy to pass through. My brother sent money home when he could.

"Finally, we were approved to leave Afghanistan. The International Rescue Committee [IRC] gave us airfare, which we repaid six months later, as required.[6] Someone from IRC was waiting for us at the airport in Atlanta and brought us to an apartment in Clarkston. The IRC helps with rent and utilities for three to six months. They help find you a job, but no one would hire Mohammad. He filled out application after application—for working in a chicken factory, washing dishes, being a hotel worker. He took drug tests and went to interviews. The IRC would call and say, they didn't hire you. In Afghanistan, Mohammad worked for the United States for eleven years, and then there was no job for him here.

"Denise found him a job as a mechanic. Just the owner and Mohammad worked together at a repair place in Peachtree City.[7] The owner said he hired Mohammad because he had served the US military, and because he had a family. The owner trained Mohammad, who went from zero mechanical ability to eighty percent very quickly. It was a good job but an hour and a half drive each way. After a year, Mohammad had to quit because the job was so far from home. The owner cried when Mohammad told him he was leaving and said he should move his family closer to Peachtree City. But there is no mosque there and no grocery that sells halal—meat blessed in God's name when the animal is sacrificed and bled.

"We met Denise at our apartment community in Clarkston soon after we moved in. Mohammad saw her stop outside the apartment of an Iraqi woman. Women were gathered around her, talking. She had lots of handbags with her. Mohammad asked the women to bring Denise to talk with us the next time she came. After a couple of weeks I started training, and four months later

Denise gave me a sewing machine to work from home. Until I met her, I cried every day because I felt so lonely and helpless. After Denise, I was busy and earning money. I didn't drive at the time, so Mohammad dropped off my finished work and picked up new patterns. Then I took driving lessons and got my driver's license.

"One day several months ago, I couldn't breathe normally. Mohammad took me to the family doctor who said I had a sore throat. He gave me some medicine and sent me home. After two days, I was so weak I fell to the floor and my breathing was worse. Mohammad called the doctor who told us to go to the emergency room. I had pneumonia and was checked into the hospital so they could give me medicine through an IV tube."

Here, Mohammad took over the story. He told me he had their baby with him at the hospital and that upstairs neighbors had looked after the other children. The hospital staff said he should go home because Fahima would be in the hospital for one or two days. But at 5 a.m., the hospital called and told him Fahima was worse. Mohammad related a troubling time.

"They said, 'We're taking her to ICU [intensive care unit]. She needs oxygen.' I didn't understand and said I wanted to talk to the doctor. They said, 'We don't have time. Your wife could die.' I went to the hospital with the baby, and my neighbors took the older children to the bus for school.

"Fahima's lungs didn't work. She was on machines and was in a coma for nine days. Then an X-ray showed the pneumonia was gone, and they took out the tube. She was fine for one day, but then her breathing slowed down again. The doctors said the pneumonia had come back, worse than before. They put her to sleep, did a CT scan, and found she had a blood clot in her lung.

"Denise found an Afghan doctor who could explain things to us in our language. The doctor called Fahima's parents in Afghanistan and explained her condition. I had started a new job but had to quit because the children couldn't be left alone and the baby needed care. We have no family to help us here.

"Fahima was in the ICU for nineteen more days—a total of thirty-two days. After she left the hospital, she had many doctor appointments. I filed for unemployment and gave proof that Fahima had been in the hospital. I borrowed money from friends to pay the rent. Family and Children Services gave us food stamps and Medicaid. Then nine months later, Fahima had pain in her chest, and once again, she couldn't breathe. The doctor took out her tonsils and she's much better now.

"When Fahima recovered, I got a job as a cross-country truck driver for an Indian company. I would drive my car to Manassas, Virginia, and begin driving from there. I was on the road for a month to a month and a half and made only a few hundred dollars more than I did in Kabul. As the oldest son, I'm expected to support my parents who are old now. Every month I send some money, but not as much as I wish I could. Now I have left driving and I'm looking for other work.

"I applied for citizenship, which costs $640 for the citizen application and $85 for the biometrics fee.[8] Before we came here, we were checked by Homeland Security, the CIA, the FBI, and two other agencies. Now, more checks."

Mohammad sat back and Fahima resumed her story.

"Because Mohammad was gone for so long, I learned to drive. For a while, I picked up and delivered my work to Peace of Thread. I went to Clarkston two or three times a week until I was pregnant. Now I call when I'm finished sewing, and Denise or Stephanie picks up the work. When I lived in Clarkston, I helped at the weekend sales events. My pay varies. Sometimes I get $100 a month, sometimes $400, sometimes $50. If someone buys a handbag I made, I get half the sales price. Now, because I'm alone with the children, I sew when I have time.

"When I was in the hospital, Denise visited me every day. She is a good woman and a good friend. Before I met her, I had no friend here. She comes to visit me even now. That means a lot to me. Denise helps us in many ways. We want our children to go to the best schools, and Denise told us where to look for a house. We found an acceptable house needing repair. A friend of Mohammad's cosigned for the loan. My health is better now, and Mohammad has returned to work for the trucking company."

Nasima:
The Price of Education

Let brotherly love continue.
Be not forgetful to entertain strangers: for thereby some
have entertained angels unawares.
Remember them that are in bonds, as bound with them;
and them which suffer adversity, as being yourselves also in
the body.
　—Hebrews 13:1-3

RECENTLY, DENISE NEEDED A WOMAN who could interpret for Peace of Thread's Afghan threaders who speak Dari or Pashto. I called the resettlement agency, World Relief, and asked for a referral to an interpreter. I was put in touch with Nasima, who came to the United States from Afghanistan two years ago to study law.

Nasima speaks the main languages of her native country, but when I spoke with her by phone, I found she was truly gifted in English as well. Now that Nasima is acquainted with Peace of Thread, she too is hooked on its mission and committed to serving as a volunteer interpreter.

Nasima is twenty-five years old. She was born into and lived through turbulent years in Afghanistan. Knowing how difficult her life must've been, I wanted to spend some time with her, hear about her life, and ask how she came to be in Atlanta studying at Emory University. We arranged to meet on campus after one of her classes.

When I arrived at our meeting place, I recognized her immediately: a slender young woman of medium height with long dark hair and deep brown eyes. We took to each other right away, and she generously added to my understanding of her country by sharing details of her life. This is what she told me.

"I was born in the capital, Kabul, a city crowded with people who fled the provinces only to find themselves in the center of conflict, a battleground for tribal wars. Surviving hunger is the main occupation in the city, and success at that is a matter of chance, not hard work. Kabul is the only hope for Afghanistan, yet its streets are filled with handicapped and orphaned children and widows begging for a meal. Poverty is so great that families who used to care for widows and orphans now leave them to fend for themselves.

"Almost a million people were displaced by war. Many of them fled to Pakistan or Iran. Now they're coming back to Kabul only to find water, telephone, and sewage systems destroyed, little to no electricity, and forty percent unemployment. Almost half the returnees are young men under eighteen. What will they do without work? Schools were bombed, teachers were killed, and many children have never been to school. I grieve for my country."

Nasima's father and mother were born and grew up in a tiny village in Ghazni, a province of Afghanistan. Both their families had cows and sold cheese, butter, milk, and yogurt in the nearby capital of the province. The families grew wheat, as did many of their neighbors, and irrigated their crops with water from the river that ran through the village.

Nasima's parents married when her mother was seventeen and her father nineteen. Because their families were very poor, they had no money for a wedding reception after the dowry was paid. In their home, Nasima's parents had a bedroom, but with relatives and their children, twenty people occupied the house. Children slept on the floor of the main room.

Cooking was done outside, whatever the weather, on a hip-high round brick stove, by burning animal dung bolstered with a few sticks of wood. With only a small awning overhead to protect them, women cooked the main staples: cow, lamb, or goat meat, bread, and green tea. Grapes, in season, were the only fruit. When a meal was ready, the men ate first and the women waited.

Nasima, who is the fourth child, has four sisters and two brothers. Her father believed in education—at great cost to the family.

"When my oldest sister was born, my father announced to all the relatives that he would educate his daughter. My parents' extended families responded by telling them they no longer belonged to the family and that they must leave the village and take nothing with them. My mother had only two precious items: a sewing machine given to her by her mother as a wedding present, and a small prayer rug made by her grandmother. Her family refused to let her have them.

"My parents left with nothing but a small suitcase, a few dollars, and the understanding that they would never see their families again. This is the price they paid for equality for their daughters. When I was young, I didn't understand what they'd given up, and my sisters and I asked many questions. When my friends celebrated Eid and other holidays, all their relatives came to their houses. I asked my mother why no one knocked on our door for the holiday, and she never gave me a clear answer. Maybe she didn't want us to know how cruel our culture could be.

"My parents moved into a shabby room in Kabul, where it was freezing cold because buildings are made of brick. My mother was used to the mud houses in her village, which stayed warm. My parents moved again and again to cheaper and cheaper places, and each time, my mother had the walls washed and the room made livable. My parents had no furniture—nothing. My mother had only two dresses. The sacrifices my parents made so their children could be educated can't be measured.

"Over time, the remnants of war decorated nearly every corner in Kabul. In one such corner, my family lived in a one-bedroom apartment rented for the equivalent of US $50 per month. In the bedroom, we had an old bed a neighbor gave us before she fled the country. Another friend gave us china and silverware.

"We had a small kitchen that had a few utilities, but there was no oven or refrigerator. The stove required attachment to a portable gas tank that sat on a small wooden stool. We refilled it monthly at a nearby gas station. The corners of our kitchen table were swollen because of water leakage. The kitchen window was a bit high, and I used to take a stool when my mother wasn't looking and watch boys playing football on the playground below. Girls weren't allowed to go there.

"Like everyone in my family, I had one outfit. It was black. I had one headscarf that was white and two pairs of shoes. My mother faithfully washed our clothes by hand and kept us clean. Eventually, she saved enough money for a small, electric washing machine from Germany, but we so seldom had electricity in Kabul that it was of little use. We didn't care that our clothes didn't fit, and we loved to look at them after my mother washed them because they looked shiny and new.

"My father got a job teaching physics at a university. He'd gone to school to become a teacher, and he received a scholarship to study in Russia for his master's degree. My mother had never been to school, but she believed as strongly as my father did that not only her sons but her daughters should be educated.

"My father's monthly salary was very small—about US $200 to $300. His salary was only enough to put food on the table, and very little of that. Once I asked my father why he didn't become a doctor and make more money. He said, 'I'm from a village. My teacher was so important to me, and being able to teach people was a dream come true for me.'

"My father was always concerned that we eat healthy food and be healthy. He wouldn't leave for work each day until he'd watched us drink our milk. He made sure my mother gave us fruit, vegetables, and plenty of water. My mother got us to eat fruit by saying it made our skin beautiful, and she told us to eat slowly because that made us beautiful too.

"Our custom is to eat on the floor with a cloth spread out and the pots set on it. We eat with our right hand. Some adults have a plate and a spoon, but that wasn't so in our family. As children, each of us had a plate, a spoon, and our own cup. My mother had us wear gloves to wash the dishes. She showed us her hands and told us that wearing gloves would keep our hands from looking like hers.

"My mother couldn't go out even to shop for food unless a man was with her. If we ran out of something, she had to wait until my father came home. Then all of us would go to the store together.

"One day when my father took me for an appointment, I told him how hungry I was. He bought me a kabob and sat at the table with me, eating nothing. When I asked him why he wasn't eating, he said he was full. A stranger passed by and said my father would surely go to paradise because he would do without to feed his child.

"My father celebrated our birthdays, even though Afghanis don't. We all received one small thing to commemorate our birthday.

"Food was an issue when I was young, as it is now. Because of a lack of security, we can't import or export food items. Let's say a farmer wants to take a load of apples to Pakistan. Along the way, different groups will be fighting. The trucks will be halted. They may sit for a week, and the apples will rot. Or the truck will get to the border and an armed group will demand money. If no payment is made, the armed men will make the truck turn around, or they might kill the driver and take the truck. We have fruits, vegetables, and carpets to export, but we can't cross the border."

Nasima told me about the different lives of boys and girls.

"For girls, when you know your right hand from your left, you learn cooking and cleaning, and then you get married. Girls play with dolls until they're five or six, and they are often married as young as thirteen to much older men. Boys play even less than girls do, and many of them don't attend school either. As soon as boys know their right hand from their left, they start working with their fathers in the fields to learn how to make money."

I asked Nasima how women who can't read or write learn the Qu'ran. She believes the messages in the Qu'ran are cultural, not religious.

"How do we make this woman a Muslim? The mullah teaches the women and children the five prayers to say each day. They memorize. There is no discussion of meaning. If women could read and write, they would know their rights, and that's why they are kept from school."

Nasima said that schools are structured differently in Afghanistan than they are in the United States.

"From first to third grade, boys and girls are in the same class, but in different sections. From fourth through tenth grade, they go to separate schools. Eleventh and twelfth grade are considered college. Law school is another four years.

"My public school was near the apartment, and it was considered one of the best in the city. There was no tuition, and books were provided. We did have to pay for our supplies. I can't describe the happiness and the fear I felt on the day my father enrolled my brother and me in first grade. We ended up in the same class, but we didn't sit together. We were separated into the girls' and boys' sections. I was elated to have a crisp new notebook with lots of white pages to fill. I wanted to write the world in it, to fill every inch, but I had no idea where to start.

"My incentive to study hard and become educated was because my father always told me that one day I would become a 'big woman'. In my mind, that meant I'd wear high heels and would be the teacher instead of the student. I was mature for my age, and I liked to take on the role of an adult.

"Despite struggling with poverty and war, my father made sure that inside our house we had peace and happiness. Four walls can't block out a world of misery and adversity, and some unpleasant memories stay with me. The sound of a jet was the alarm. My mother would shout, 'Run, run to the basement.' By the time we were halfway down the stairs, we'd be joined by other tenants rushing and squeezing to make it to the common area for ten apartments. The jets would start dropping bombs, and my heart would drop to my stomach. My hands would go numb. I was so thankful that we lived on the first floor, and I bragged to my friends that we could make it to the basement before anyone else.

"No matter the chaos, I never forgot my storybook. When everyone else was closing their eyes and holding their hands over their ears, I'd cope with my fear by reading my stories. But my book was half burnt from a bomb that hit our bookcase and burnt most the books and some toys. I played with the toy remnants and wrote on the empty margins of the burnt notebooks. My favorite toy was a yellow dog that had its tail cut off. My mother mended it for me because the insides kept coming out.

"One of my saddest memories is that I lost the shoes my father gave me as a reward for my high exam score. They were my favorite things because they had bows, and my heels made a clicking sound when I walked. I made the mistake of wearing them to the mosque for my religious studies class so I could show them to my friends. During class, I worried that someone would step on them. I ran to the shoe rack right after class. They'd been stolen. I cried my broken heart out and walked home barefoot that day.

"My family had no money for trips or entertainment, so our days were much the same. We went to school, came home, studied, and read. I went outside to play with my friends, but we didn't have a ball or a jump rope. I'd invite my friends in, and we'd practice putting makeup on each other or we'd cook together.

"My father taught all his children the basics of the English language. He pushed me to read books in English and to talk to him about what I'd learned. In the same way, I learned Farsi, Hindi, and Arabic, which I understand better than I speak."

Nasima was in law school in Afghanistan before she came to the United States. The classes included men and women, except for those about Sharia law. She found the school disappointing.

"Kabul University is the only state institution for higher education, and it is the best in the country," she said. "I expected it to be a step above public school. Instead it was two stories of unpainted walls, dark and dingy hallways, and disrepair. Windows were smashed. Doors to our classrooms were broken. Despite the shabbiness of our surroundings, we expected understanding and assistance from our professors. They rarely communicated with us, and when they did, it was in an arrogant manner. They did prepare me to ask challenging questions.

"The difference between my professors in Afghanistan and my professors here is profound. I can't compare the academic environment in Afghanistan with what I'm experiencing here. I'm so lucky to be part of this educational system. It has developed in me a love of all humanity, respect for diversity, and appreciation for the practice of welcoming people."

I wondered how Nasima had managed to get enrolled at Emory.

"I sat for an examination with fifty people who qualified to take the test. I received the highest score, and I was hired by the US State Department for its office in Kabul. Almost immediately, I put in a request for a Special Immigrant Visa to come to the United States. Even though I was working for your country, it took eight months to process my request. At the same time, I received a diversity scholarship from Emory University. Now I'm a permanent resident, and I'll apply for citizenship."

Nasima shares an apartment with a brother who was already living in Atlanta, but her other sisters and brothers live in Afghanistan.

"My brother here treats me like a princess. He has a law degree from Afghanistan and a master's in law from Emory. I have one sister in medical school and one in law school. One is a journalist and one is in high school. My married brother is a freelance journalist. His life has been threatened because he writes and broadcasts about the Taliban for the BBC, Turkish TV, and Kabul TV. Despite the risk in challenging cultural norms and religious beliefs, he gives voice to the women of Afghanistan through his reporting. Life in the United States is so different. Women can travel, create their own futures, and express their thoughts freely. I don't know if they realize how fortunate they are."

I asked Nasima what had attracted her to law.

"We all deserve to live in peace and harmony," she said. "I would like to see equality and justice for women, and I know there's much to be done. The treatment of women in Afghanistan continues to be feudal."

Would she like to return to Afghanistan?

"Of course, I miss my parents very much. My father used to read all the time, but now his eyes are too weak. My mother has rheumatism.

"Afghanistan remains a very dangerous place. Car and suicide bombings continue in the heart of Kabul and elsewhere. The country is sunk in corruption, warlords rule vast swaths of the country, and the rule of law is declining. All those challenges make it nearly impossible for a woman to be safe. None of us can speak out publicly until we are allowed to speak in our own homes. When women have constitutional protection and security, I'll return to Afghanistan.

"Meanwhile, I want to practice immigration law here. I know what it's like to leave everything and everyone behind. I want to help other women who come here looking for a peaceful place to thrive."

Nasima is a powerful addition to the refugee women and the volunteers at Peace of Thread.

Memphis:
New Threaders, New Patterns

"Now which of these three would you say was a neighbor to
the man who was attacked by bandits?" Jesus asked.
The man replied, "The one who showed him mercy."
Then Jesus said, "Yes, now go and do the same."
—Luke 10:36-37

In 2009, Renee Lamb, a lifelong resident of northwest Mississippi, prepared to make her third mission trip to Lebanon. In communicating with Operation Mobilization about its humanitarian work, she was put in contact with Denise Smith, who was living in Aley, Lebanon, a year into her work there. The two women communicated by email about future work they might do together. Soon, they shared their faith experience and the inner peace they gained by serving people in need. Later that year, the two women met.

"At the time, I was volunteering with a team from Heart for Lebanon in the hills outside Beirut," Renee said. "We were among several groups housed at a Catholic convent. From there, we distributed food and clothing to Syrian refugees who were living nearby in pathetically inadequate conditions. Seven people might live in a building's janitor closet or in a bombed and abandoned building.[1]

"One day I was at church in Beirut with a contact I'd made at Heart for Lebanon. She said she was on her way to have lunch at Denise Smith's house. This was my chance to meet the woman I'd come to know by email, so I invited myself along. Denise greeted me warmly and brought me up to date with her life and her plans. Since that meeting my relationship with Denise has deepened, and she eventually inspired me to create a chapter of Peace of Thread near me—in Memphis, Tennessee."

Renee's family goes back generations in Hernando, Mississippi, just a half hour highway drive from Memphis.

"We lived in the country," Renee told me, "and my grandfather helped build the small community church we attended. My life was uneventful until I reached my last year of high school."

Breaking Bread Together

In 1984, Renee graduated high school at seventeen, married, and moved with her husband—a military man—to Biloxi, Mississippi, and then to Turkey. I wondered if the young Renee might have found the change to such a foreign culture strange, intimidating, or in any way difficult.

"Those years in Turkey were three of the best years of my young life," Renee told me. "For the first time, I met people who were Muslim. I was exposed to different religions and languages around the military communities in Izmir, Ankara, and Adana."

Shortly after returning to the United States in 1989, Renee and her husband divorced, which made Renee the single mother of their two young children—a son, Cory, and a daughter, Cally.

"I got a job as a UPS driver in Hernando and enlisted my mother, who lived nearby, to care for my children while I was working. In 1994, I met Danny, the man I've been married to for more than twenty years. He adopted my children, and we had a daughter, Hailey."

In 1999, Renee opened a retail store for party goods in Hernando, and she succeeded in business for about eight years—until a superstore and a national franchise moved into the area, making it impossible for her to compete on pricing.

"After closing the store, I was eager for another mission trip. I went to Istanbul, Turkey, for two weeks with Campus Crusade. When I returned, I was more mature, and I developed friendships that continue to this day."

In 2008, Renee again returned to Turkey with Danny and Hailey, who was thirteen at the time.

"Danny supports me in this," Renee said. "His father was a deacon and his mother a church secretary. He had a good foundation and he's active in our church. The first time I was leaving for a third-world country without him, church members questioned him. But he'd say, 'Who am I to get between her and God?' Danny never held me back. When I see a need, I choose to respond with my money and the gifts God has given me."

In her first attempt at a service trip with a faith group, back in 2003, Renee met with disappointment. At the time, US and allied forces had attacked Iraq and set off a war that involved US troops until 2011.[2] Soon after the war started, Renee's church began to collect supplies for the Iraqi people.

"Each box of food weighed sixty pounds," Renee said. "The box was filled with a variety of staples such as flour, sugar, tea, and other nonperishable items. Church members would bring the supplies to a church, where they were shipped to the coast and then shipped to Iraq for pickup by the International Missions Board."

Renee was among a group of Americans who bravely volunteered to go into Iraq and help deliver supplies to Iraqi people whose access to basic products was affected by the conflict.

"Then the Jordanian embassy was bombed," Renee said, "and no volunteers for the International Missions Board were allowed to go.[3] I was so disappointed. I'd found something to do that would help women and children in a war-torn place and keep me in touch with the Middle Eastern culture I'd grown to love."

Instead, in 2004 and 2005, Renee joined ten-day trips to Lebanon her church organized. The first year, her assignment was to teach professional women how a business is started in the United States. The next year, she taught a Bible curriculum to children in a Druze community in Aley, Lebanon.

"We flew into Beirut," Renee said, "and we were driven up into the mountains. I stayed in an old hospital in Aley, which had been bombed. So much of the town had been destroyed, and families had moved into abandoned houses scarred by bullet holes.

"I guess I can't really explain why I came to love the Middle East so much, except that I always felt at home there. I learned a few words and greetings in Arabic, but I always had an interpreter."

After her service in Turkey and Lebanon, Renee read a book by a Baptist pastor in the United States.[4] In the book, she told me, the pastor challenges readers to walk their faith, and he asks them to list places where they'd like to go and where they'd *not* want to go.

"I said to myself, Africa and Asia. But then I read on, and the pastor said to start praying for where you don't want to go."

In 2011, Renee was part of her church's ten-day mission trip to Uganda in East Africa. She found her living conditions highly uncomfortable but thrived on the landscape, the personal interaction, and her belief in fulfilling a mission.

"We flew into Entebbe [central Uganda] and drove to Kisoro near the border with Rwanda and Congo. The landscape was mountainous, lush, and green with coffee and banana plantations. We passed through jungle, and the drive was timed so we were out of it before sunset. A breakdown after dark could've been dangerous. Without access to a car repair shop, we would've been vulnerable to animals as well as people who might've wanted to take advantage of foreigners in a compromised position.

"We arrived at a small hotel where the door to my room was about three inches too short at the bottom, which I was afraid would allow wildlife to wander in at night. I had brought peanut butter, crackers, and other snacks with me, and I kept them in a plastic container. That was after a mouse ate through the baggie I'd carried them in. The showers were cold.

"Our job was to teach and encourage local women who already believed in Christ. We sat on the floors of thatched-roof houses, shared food and drink, and talked about the Bible. In an open-air building, village women listened to our stories and sang with us."

Renee was moved by the women she met.

"The women of Uganda were beautiful inside and out. Although they had little in monetary terms, they were probably the happiest people I ever met. That kind of attitude makes you rethink the idea that having more stuff will make you happy. They had found happiness, which encouraged me to do the same."

Since their meeting in Beirut in 2009, Renee and Denise had continued to exchange emails. In 2012, Denise, now reestablished in the States, called Renee and left a phone message for her. Renee, busy with family commitments at the time, postponed calling Denise back. In the meantime, Renee, who was still searching for ways to help the Iraqi people, learned that Catholic Charities was sponsoring incoming Iraqi refugees. Renee called Catholic Charities and met with an official who informed her that the incoming refugees were from Africa and Nepal.

"It was like Uganda," Renee said. "Pray for where you don't want to go."

People at the charity suggested to Renee that she organize a Thanksgiving dinner. First, she drove to an appointment with one of the organization's coordinators, but before she got out of the car Denise called again, and introduced her to the concept and the reality of Peace of Thread. She told Renee about her project and how it was beginning to evolve.

"My mind was whirling," Renee said, "After my meeting with the Catholic Charities coordinator, I asked myself, 'How will I do all this?'"

In June of 2013, Renee started the Memphis chapter of Peace of Thread.

"Well, that's when we had our first meetings. When Denise and her staff arrived in Memphis to help us, things were not where we wanted them to be. We didn't have threaders or sewing machines. We went to a local apartment complex to find women interested in sewing. The next day, we had about twenty-five women from Nepal and all over Africa. Since then, many of the women have found me through word of mouth.

"The irony is that I don't know how to sew," Renee confessed. "My volunteers are the teachers. My job is to care for the refugee women in the same way Denise does. I speak at churches and other places to recruit volunteers and to discover more threaders."

Three years after I first met Renee at Denise's outpost northeast of Atlanta,

Renee Lamb, Memphis Director

I joined Denise and her core team on a visit to the Memphis chapter. The team wanted to review inventory, design new bags, and meet with threaders and volunteers to exchange ideas.

On the way to the Peace of Thread Memphis training center, we pulled up to an apartment unit in a subsidized housing area to visit with Habiba, a woman from Somalia who is one of the chapter's threaders. I had asked to meet and talk with a few refugee women to hear their stories and learn how they contribute to Peace of Thread Memphis.

Habiba's daughter, Fatima, who's in her mid-twenties, opened the door for us and showed us into the living area, which was furnished with two small sofas and some wooden chairs. The windows were covered with flowered sheets that blocked the glare of the sun but also made the room dim. Both women wore carefully tied headscarves, long skirts, and cotton tops in subdued colors. They had prepared fried chicken, which was waiting in a large aluminum cooking pot set on one of the chairs.

Habiba's command of English is minimal, so Fatima served as interpreter until she left for work. Later I learned that Habiba had avoided answering some questions because she was reluctant for her daughter to know the stories of her life. Back in Atlanta, I recruited a local bilingual woman who spoke to Habiba by telephone, asked my questions, and then shared her responses with me. Habiba's story is the product of both interviews.

"I was born in Kurtun, Somalia, in about 1973.[5] My mother, who now lives in Mogadishu, had two girls and two boys. In my culture, children didn't go to school. Girls stayed in the home and cooked and cleaned. Boys worked on the farm. We had fifteen cows, and we grew watermelon, onions, corn, and tomatoes. When we had enough corn, we sold some of it. Otherwise, we used everything we grew for our own food. Life was hard.

"I was first married at age thirteen to a twenty-eight-year-old man in an arranged marriage. In our culture, girls get married when they reach puberty. There was no bride price. I could not refuse. I had no voice about my life.

"My husband's parents had died, so he moved into our house. He was kind and helpful, open to everyone and very loving. My father died when I was about twenty-five, and my husband helped my sisters, my brothers, and my mother.

"In 1991, Somalis started fighting each other.[6] When my baby was eight months old, the war came to our house. Everyone—including doctors, store owners, and farmers—was running. The militia shot my husband. The fighters slapped my face so hard, I almost fell, but I ran. I had to run because

I didn't want to die. After we fled, we didn't have enough food. My baby was sick, but there were no doctors and there was no medicine, so my baby died.

"I went to Dadaab, Kenya, where UNHCR had set up Ifo refugee camp.[7] Now, with the addition of a second camp—Ifo2—and two more camps—Hagadera and Dagahaley—it is the largest refugee camp in the world. I was safe living in the camp, and I had enough food to survive day by day.

"I lived in Ifo for eighteen years—from 1991 to 2009—and I met my second husband in the refugee camp. A holy man came to bless our marriage. People gathered and we had a party. My husband worked in the camp fetching water with a wheelbarrow for the neighbors. He earned 8,000 Kenyan shillings per month, enough to buy meat and food for our children in addition to what was distributed.[8]

"I learned about cleaning jobs from my friends, and I worked for other refugees in the camp. For a small amount, I painted their houses with a mixture of clay and manure. Fatima, my oldest daughter, and my mother cared for my five boys while I worked.

"Our family slept on a rug on the floor. To cook our food, we piled four rocks in a circle and put three wooden sticks on top. We used a flint to start the fire and added a little gas to keep it going. We made our main food in a big black pot. We boiled rice or potatoes, corn and cabbage with a little lamb or goat. We ate bananas and macaroni, we drank tea, and we baked bread over the fire on a flat sheet.

"With money we saved from selling water and from my cleaning, we bought a little store in the camp. It supplied us with sugar, milk, and soap for the children. We fixed up the house that the organization gave us with the help of an uncle. We had three rooms. My husband and I slept in one room. My mother, Fatima, and the boys slept in the other. We gathered in the third room. The kitchen and bathroom were outdoors. My uncle lived elsewhere, but he came to help with the house. Then he, one sister, and one brother came to live with us.

"We received a food ration every fifteen days. The box had flour, milk, and eggs, or rice and beans, or tomatoes, beef, camel milk, and camel meat. Sometimes there was goat meat. We cooked in the morning and went to work in the store. We had no money for lunch. We watched our food ration carefully because if we finished it too soon, we'd have to wait for days until the next distribution. Once a week, we might have a little beef, beans, macaroni. People died all around us from cholera, malaria.

"Everyone is issued a food card. Some people sold their food and then had nothing until the next month. When a family was resettled, the United

Nations took away its food card and gave it to another refugee. Refugees were sent to Canada, England, Australia, and the United States.

"The Kenyan government would not allow refugees to work in the camp unless they spoke English or Swahili. I couldn't afford the tuition fee for classes.

"We had to fetch our water five or six times a day. The well was almost a half-mile away, and carrying the buckets was so tiring. We attached a strap to the container and looped it around our foreheads so we could carry water on our backs. Clothes had to be washed by hand every day. My husband and my daughter helped. We put soap on the clothes and then rubbed them to get the dirt out, then rinsed them in a pail of water and hung them up to dry.

"I never dreamed of going to America, and I didn't know anything about Memphis. When our name came up for resettlement, my mother went back to Somalia with two sisters and two brothers because they weren't authorized to go with us.

"I think of the days when my father brought corn from the field to the house to cook. I miss my mother. I've embraced the hand that has been dealt to me. Of course, I'd rather be in my country with my mother, but there is constant war, and there has been famine for many years as well.

"We were resettled here in a small apartment with our nine children. In 2014 we moved to this five-bedroom apartment in subsidized housing. The mosque is a long way away, so I pray at home. I go to English and naturalization classes, and I learn from television. I have seven boys and two girls. Six of my children go to school, and my four-year old stays with me.

"Now my husband works in maintenance. Fatima works at a warehouse in inventory control, and one son is a security guard at a grocery store. They all help support our family. One of our beds was supplied by the refugee service, but my husband bought the rest.

"A typical day in my house begins with soup and bread for breakfast. Lunch is at 2:15, when the children get home from school. We have meat, rice, salad, and fruit. Dinner is at seven. We have rice or macaroni, bread with peanut butter and jelly, milk or juice.

"Summer is way too hot. The children stay in and do homework, watch television, play games, sleep, or text. There's too much texting. The boys like to play with cars. We have a car. We can go to the park for a picnic or go to a playground.

"When the government aid stopped at the end of eight months, I thought we would be homeless. Thank goodness my husband got a job and works every day. We have a roof over our head, and I'm learning English. My life is stable, and I have enough food for my family. I love America because

Stephanie Marbut and Bitsy Pitts

my children have free education and I have high hopes for them. They can become pilots or engineers or doctors.

"I heard about Renee's sewing through Catholic Charities and friends. Renee came to my house to give me information about the program, and I started sewing right away. Renee brought me a sewing machine and my supplies. I can help the family now. I want to be a sewing teacher for Peace of Thread."

The night before we left Memphis, Renee and Denise took a lamp to Habiba's home and moved her sewing machine away from the living area window. Shots had been fired in the neighborhood just days before. Since our visit, I learned that Habiba and her family have moved to a home built by Habitat for Humanity.

After spending time with Habiba, we continued on our way to Peace of Thread Memphis, housed on the second floor of the gymnasium at the First Baptist Church.

We entered a spacious room, where fabric could be easily organized in the rows of shelves that lined one long wall. Windows on the other side of the room looked over the roof of the sanctuary. The cutting tables were big enough for four women at a time to design, cut, and pin fabric, and for teacher and student to work together. An under-the-counter refrigerator stored bottled water and soda, and a play area was set up for visiting children. One of the threaders was waiting to talk with me.

Aminata, from the Democratic Republic of the Congo, speaks French and Kikongo but only a little English. As a middle-aged woman, English doesn't come easily to her. After an unsuccessful attempt at communication, I reserved a telephone interview with her and sought out an interpreter. Back in Atlanta, I enlisted a multilingual immigration specialist who asked my questions of Aminata and explained her answers to me.

"I was born in 1962, one of eight children born to a wealthy farmer and livestock breeder and his wife. My father raised and sold sheep, beef cattle, and chickens. My five brothers helped with the livestock and worked with my father in the fields growing cola fruit.

"I wasn't allowed to work outside. My grandfather said all girls must stay inside so they aren't tempted to play with boys. My two sisters and I learned the household duties we'd need to know as wives and mothers. We played dress up, jumped rope, and sang songs with the neighbor girls, and we cared for the younger children. I never went to school, so I can't read or write, but I learned the Qur'an and prayed with my family.

"At fifteen, I was married to a twenty-one-year-old man. It wasn't an arranged marriage. My husband fell in love with me and came to my family to ask for my hand. Because his father was also wealthy, the dowry was substantial. My wedding was a joyful celebration of food and dance. Henna was painted on my hands, and I wore a white blouse, a traditional long skirt, a turban, and many handmade bead necklaces.

"With my husband, I moved to a two-room house with detached kitchen and bathroom. My husband went to different towns, bought goods, and brought them back to Brazzaville to sell in his small store. He was a quiet man and did well. My life was peaceful until I was about thirty-five and civil war came to my town. People were killed like animals, and we had no choice but to flee. Thousands of people left Congo for Gabon.

"At that time, I had seven children—newborn to age fourteen. When militias came, five of my children were visiting my mother and father in another area. They fled to Mali and ended up in a refugee camp.

"My sister and my father were killed, but there was no time to mourn the dead. I ran with my husband, my baby, and one of my older daughters. If we had stayed, my children and I would've been killed as well. I was shot in the left leg, and I injured the right one when I fell. In the chaos, we became separated from my husband, and I never saw him again.

"We were told we'd be safe at a Catholic church in Gabon, but when we got there, we found villagers standing outside the church cursing us and telling us to go home. At first food was cooked for us, but after a while we made our own food outside over a fire, like everyone else. People slept on mattresses on the floor, almost nose to nose.

"After some time, a charitable organization gave us some rent money. With my daughters, I went to Libreville in Gabon to live, and I learned I had diabetes. There was no money to pay for treatment, but my illness made me eligible for asylum in another country.

"Now I live in Memphis with a niece who came here to go to college. My daughters are American citizens. One is in college and lives on campus. My other daughter fixes computers. She is married to a man from Senegal and has two children.

"I haven't seen my mother or my five other children since 1997. A refugee agency helped me find my children, and I keep in touch with them by phone. Two sons and one daughter are in Mali, one daughter is in Congo, and one son is in Gabon. My mother had a stroke in 2013 and is paralyzed on her left side. Three of my brothers are in Mali, and one is in Congo. I don't know about the others.

"My children grew up without me and I miss them. I must be an American citizen to ask to bring them here, but I can't read or write, and I can't afford an immigration lawyer. I sew for Peace of Thread but I can go only once a week. I wish I had a sewing machine at home."

When Denise, her team, and I arrived to see the Memphis chapter, it was late at night, and we went straight to bed at Renee's home in Hernando. We woke early to a hot breakfast, despite Denise and Renee having talked until two in the morning. Renee's kitchen is a gathering place, and her daughter Cally and her three children were at the table being served. The view from the dining area was serene. Renee lives in the countryside, on three acres that include a pond, mature trees, a spacious covered patio, and an inviting pool. Like Denise, Renee is a caretaker. She delivers her grandchildren to a sitter and to preschool before she begins her own daily rounds.

"I decided to start this chapter of Peace of Thread," Renee said, "because I long to help the international community. The sewing projects give me a great way to be a part of the women's daily lives."

Renee believes these women need someone to help them find their voice, and Renee herself isn't shy about speaking up, as she demonstrated a few years back.

"St. Jude's Children's Research Hospital was having a special guest visit the hospital. When I learned that [now former First Lady] Michelle Obama would attend, I wrote and asked for five minutes with her. I wanted to tell her about Peace of Thread and give her one of our handbags. I figured if I could talk to Jesus every day, I could talk to the wife of a US president."

Renee's plan didn't turn out exactly as she had hoped.

"I didn't see Mrs. Obama, but the State Department retweeted an article the local paper wrote about Peace of Thread. A few weeks later, I got a letter from Mrs. Obama thanking us for our work. I thought she'd never see it, but I think she did, and that makes me happy."

For Renee, a typical day begins at 5:30 in the morning, when she prepares breakfast for her husband, her daughter, and her grandchildren, who are left with Renee when her daughter goes to work. She takes her grandchildren to day care and then continues to Memphis to work with Peace of Thread or to visit the refugee women who work as threaders. Renee returns to daycare at 3:00 to pick up her grandchildren, who stay with her until 6:00, when their mother picks them up. Despite her commitments, Renee finds time for the refugee women and the volunteers who want to be part of the Memphis threaders. Recently, Renee found some new recruits.

"I sat in on a class at Christian Brothers University. The professor told the students about Peace of Thread and how it strives to improve the lives of refugee families. Five students now want to help me as interns or volunteers. They're interested in social media, web design, and teaching.

"Information also went to a job counselor at the University of Memphis College of Art in the hope of getting interns to design handbags for women ages eighteen to thirty-four. My volunteers, as well as the refugee women, are much older, and our designs have been very conservative. A change will be welcomed by all of us."

Regardless of the changes that come to the lives and work of the Memphis threaders, their success seems inevitable. Renee's quiet strength, serious nature, and calm disposition make the project centered, grounded, and peaceful.

Clarkston:
One Square Global Mile

This is what the LORD says: Be fair-minded and just. Do what is right! Help those who have been robbed; rescue them from their oppressors. Quit your evil deeds! Do not mistreat foreigners, orphans, and widows.
      —Jeremiah 22:3

ONE DAY IN EARLY DECEMBER 2016, Denise invited me to the Peace of Thread Christmas party. Wanting to contribute food for a large crowd, I went shopping at a superstore near Clarkston. While loading my cart, I heard a woman speaking Arabic. I looked down the aisle and saw two young women in traditional Muslim dress studying the labels of canned goods and seeming to discuss them in depth. In Clarkston, this isn't an unusual sight. I approached them, asked them if they spoke English—which they did well enough, and asked if I could help them find anything.

I introduced myself and told them how much I love knowing people from other cultures. They were shy and understandably guarded, but after a few minutes they seemed to sense that I was harmless. They joined me at a nearby coffee shop for conversation, and after a few visits together they became my friends. The woman were sisters in their twenties from Syria. Over time, they told me how they had become refugees and how their lives had unfolded since they'd arrived in the United States.

Every refugee experience is unique, but the story of these two women is strikingly like those I've heard from other refugee women at Peace of Thread and around Clarkston. Because of similarities in refugee resettlement, I present their story as a composite of the experiences of the many women I've come to know in the Clarkston community. I use this narrative to explain to American friends what defines refugees and how elements of that definition determine refugees' futures. The archetypal story I tell about these sisters characterizes the refugee experience of thousands of people.

In my telling, the two sisters, Rana and Fahia, fled Syria in 2012 because of the country's civil war. Earlier that year, they were staying in a mountain village with their mother a couple of hours from their home in Aleppo, which had become unsafe. While they were away, their father was killed in an explosion near his workplace. Because of shelling, returning to Aleppo wasn't possible, but after a few months they hadn't found a way to support themselves in the village, and their cash was dwindling. Their relatives were barely coping with the war themselves.

While the women were considering returning to Aleppo, they learned that a refugee camp, Zaatari, had opened just over the border in Jordan. They asked a local truck driver to take them there—south, away from the fighting at the time. The women lived in the camp for three years, until they were admitted to the United States as refugees. When I met them, they had been living in Clarkston for a little more than a year.

Going to the refugee camp had given the mother and daughters some advantages: protection of their rights, access to food and water, shelter, and an in-camp economy (employment in the host country outside the camp is illegal); and the possibility of resettlement in a third country. To gain these advantages, they had waited in line for hours when they arrived at the camp to register with the United Nations High Commissioner for Refugees (UNHCR), which had set up an office there.

UNHCR is an international organization that collects information from people seeking refuge, documents their status, and makes referrals to countries that accept refugees for resettlement. Since 2016, refugees can apply for resettlement in one of thirty-seven countries, but the United States, Canada, Australia, and the Nordic countries are the top resettlement locations.[1] Refugees have no say over which country they ultimately go to. If a refugee declines an offer of resettlement in a particular country, her name goes to the end of the list, and another opportunity isn't likely to come up.

In international law, refugees are people who have fled conflict or persecution, who have crossed their national border into another country, and who can't return home because of risk to their life or liberty. If a person leaves her country for educational or economic reasons—simply for a better life—she can't be classified as a refugee. Instead, she is a migrant and not protected by the same laws.

My young friends' refugee registration meant they couldn't be forced to return to Syria while the conflict continued, and as it continued, the likelihood of their being able to return to a normal life there any time soon became remote.

As documented camp residents, the women received food cards from the United Nations World Food Program (WFP), which allowed them to purchase items from shops at the camp. The WFP is one of about twenty organizations that offer services such as education, sanitation, and medical care to residents of Zaatari. Like some long-established refugee camps, Zaatari is thankfully replete with organizations striving to make life bearable for residents. But some camps throughout the world are served by only a few humanitarian agencies able to maintain a presence in dangerous locations. At Zaatari, the International Committee of the Red Cross has a presence to help residents trace relatives who also may have fled Syria. From time to time, Rana and Fahia sought information about members of their extended family.

Despite humanitarian services, Zaatari is a place of impermanence and privation; a way station, not a hometown. Residents endure scarcity, cold, crime, extreme boredom, and other conditions that make life harsh.[2] During their three years in the camp, Rana, Fahia, and their mother lived in a tent. They were, however, able to continue learning English, thanks to volunteer instructors organized by a charitable organization. Their mother, an educated woman, found employment as a translator for one of the service organizations.

In all, life for the women was tenuous, and once the trauma of what had happened to them subsided, grief and loss replaced it. But Rana, Fahia, and their mother were lucky. They were selected for resettlement in the United States. Most years, less than one percent of the world's refugees are resettled in a new country.[3] On average, eight years pass before an opportunity for resettlement comes up, and some refugees spend decades in a camp or elsewhere in a host country, where they may marry another refugee and have children who are born stateless.

Resettlement representatives considered the women to be strong candidates for a successful life in a new country: they were young, were educated, had a good command of English, and carried themselves with dignity. They would find work in America and build new lives there.

Before they were approved for resettlement in the United States, however, they were carefully scrutinized by international and US federal agencies. Staff from UNHCR interviewed them multiple times, on alert for inconsistencies and contradictions in their story. Once they were referred to the United States, interrogators from the Department of Homeland Security also interviewed them three times, and information about them was processed through US databases, including those of the Central Intelligence Agency and other security agencies. The vetting of the mother and daughters lasted two years.

One day, the women learned they were cleared and would go to a city called Clarkston, just east of Atlanta, Georgia. They attended a cultural orientation—a crash course in life in the USA. Additional orientation would happen after they arrived. Like all refugees, before they were given the airline tickets

Artisans Hands

to their new home, the women signed a promissory note agreeing to repay the cost of their flight. The International Organization for Migration operates an interest-free loan program for these flights and reimburses the US government as refugees make payments according to a predetermined schedule.[4]

For resettlement, the women became clients of the International Rescue Committee (IRC), one of the nine US resettlement agencies with which UNHCR works. Rana, Fahia, and their mother arrived in Atlanta at night, and a representative of IRC who spoke Arabic met them at the airport, welcomed them, and drove them to a Clarkston apartment furnished with basic necessities—a used sofa, a table and four chairs, two double beds, a few dishes, and a handful of pots and pans. In the kitchen, they found a small bottle of oil, bread and jam, packets of tea, eggs, sugar—enough to get them going. Once the sun came up, the women tentatively stepped outside and began to explore their new neighborhood. As they walked through their apartment complex, they heard people speaking languages they couldn't identify.

One day, I met with Clarkston's mayor Ted Terry, and while waiting for him at Refuge Coffee shop, I too heard languages I couldn't name with confidence. When he arrived, Mayor Terry put this into perspective for me.

"We've learned that sixty languages are spoken within Clarkston," the major said. "That tells you something about the diversity of this community. About a third of our population was born outside the States."

Rana, Fahia, and their mother found a post office, a pharmacy, and a grocery store within walking distance, and they saw buses come and go on the street in front of their apartment. With help from a neighbor, they learned an essential route. They were expected to meet with their IRC caseworker on the next working day to receive basic assistance, develop an initial plan, and learn what was required of them. When they met with their caseworker—a refugee herself who had become an American citizen—they accepted that their top priority was to find work. Until then, they were expected to attend morning language classes at the IRC facility and to be at doctor appointments the caseworker would help arrange for them at the county health clinic. Young children might need immunizations before school enrollment, for example, while adults with other health conditions—such as diabetes or high blood pressure—need medication and monitoring.

Financial assistance for a transportation card, rent, utilities, and food would last for six months. After that, the family of three would be responsible for their expenses, although they might be eligible for food stamps and other assistance for low-income earners. Families with young children are generally eligible for insurance that covers the children's health care.

Sometimes, friends of mine bristle at the cost of these services to their communities, but in conversation, Bobby King, a retired director of one of the area's refugee service organizations, reminded me that the temporary assistance refugees receive comes from the federal level, not state or local governments.

"What's more," Bobby added, "nearly ninety percent of refugee households in Georgia succeed in covering their own expenses within the six-month window. Given the enormous adjustments these people have to make, I find that really impressive."

Bobby continued to explain how he thinks of this support.

"Our new residents are an investment," he said. "They do the jobs most Americans won't do. The refugee newcomers pay taxes and social security. They start businesses, and they bring a strong family work ethic that is unquantifiable. Their native languages help us in conducting global activities."

Rana and Fahia wanted to continue their education, but that would have to wait. In a few days, they received a card authorizing them to work, and IRC helped them find jobs. Three months later, they received a green card, which serves as proof of permanent residence and permission to work for ten years. Before the card expired, they could apply for citizenship (after five years' residence) or apply to renew the green card.

About three weeks after the first meeting with their caseworker, the women were given appointments for job interviews. Their command of English was sufficient to allow a few employment possibilities. Rana and Fahia both got jobs at a warehouse for household goods. When I met them, they described their work: receive boxes, stock shelves, and package outgoing items. They traveled together by bus to and from work, a long commute but during normal daytime hours, and they had their evenings free for language classes.

Their mother was not quite as fortunate. The caseworker had added her name to a list of refugee applicants for jobs at one of the poultry processing plants outside the immediate area. Many refugees who work at these plants talk about physically demanding work on assembly lines in refrigerated rooms, cutting up and packaging chickens raised in hatcheries and slaughtered for retail markets. Some workers return home with their hands stiff and cut up from the repetitive work. At least this mother from Syria would serve as a line supervisor and help translate instructions from English-speaking managers to workers who shared her language.

Rana's and Fahia's mother worked the second shift, from three in the afternoon until eleven at night. She traveled more than an hour each way in a van the processing plant operated for its refugee workers, making stops in a couple of Clarkston apartment complexes. Until they have a reliable car, many refugees work at the poultry plants because, even with the deduction from their paychecks for the company-provided transportation, the income enables them to pay the rent. Other refugees work in low-paying jobs under similar terms for nearby manufacturers of building supplies and carpeting.

Many of the refugees Denise works with at Peace of Thread are not as well off as women like Rania and Fahia. Many refugee women come from countries where education is forbidden, unaffordable, or not considered a priority for women. Some of these women have never worked outside the home or are used to different work cultures. Other refugee women have small children, and since the jobs available may be barely above minimum wage, the cost of childcare may be greater than what they can earn. In this case, the only way they can contribute to the family income is to work from home. Knowing this helps me value Peace of Thread all the more.

During their first weeks in the country, IRC staff and volunteers helped Rana and Fahia find clothes suitable for the weather. Like other resettlement agencies, IRC maintains an onsite storeroom of donated goods and a directory of thrift stores for low-cost, used clothing. The items the women found at these stores weren't what they would've worn in their native country, but only they knew how they were dressed under their hijabs and coats. They were thankful to be comfortable and warm while saving money for clothing items they might not readily find secondhand, such as good-fitting shoes.

When I first discovered Clarkston, I was confused about how it came to be populated by so many refugees and I researched its history. For decades, it was a rural, white area. Then in the 1970s, Atlanta's new international airport attracted middle-class workers, and developers built homes and apartment complexes to house an influx of residents. At that time, Clarkston was a fairly affluent community. Over the next decade, however, these residents moved on to other areas, and apartment vacancies increased. A new influx of residents who couldn't consistently pay the rent came to Clarkston. Then came crime.

In the 1990s, resettlement agencies were scouting for a core for refugee settlement. They saw that Clarkston had many qualities they were looking for, chiefly public transportation routes and low-cost housing. As refugees were resettled in the city, it became more orderly. Some landlords spruced up their buildings. Today, however, many of the apartment complexes show signs of age and wear.

Mayor Terry acknowledges that some housing is subpar.

"We have an interior code compliance regulation and an enforcement officer who spot checks," he told me. "We issue citations and take some owners to municipal court. Some complexes do attract investors who buy out slumlords. Most investors expect a high return, so rents are at market rates. But some apartment owners find compassionate capitalists, and these owners keep rents lower than others and provide add on services like a community garden. When people grow their own food and interact with each other, crime goes down."

Clarkston has issues that include policing itself.

"Police reform is hard," Mayor Terry told me. "We should provide bonuses and incentives to our police officers for learning another language and having sensitivity to different cultures. I advocate a community service officer and junior police from different cultures. We need social workers who can help solve mental health issues."

A mayor inevitably focuses on what needs improvement. I find it encouraging that residents coming from more than fifty countries live together in one small community. Maintaining harmony may mean putting aside suspicion if not hostility toward people of other religions or nations.

For Rana and Fahia, education and good jobs are priorities. They get guidance not only from IRC but also from other resettlement agencies and organizations that serve the Clarkston community. These groups offer job training and career counseling, translator accreditation, microenterprise development, financial literacy programs, youth activities, and other services. In Clarkston, residents find a state college, a technical college, and private educational facilities.

When I asked Rana and Fahia what kind of work they'd most like to do, they said they like to cook. They missed the food from Syria so much, they dreamed of opening a restaurant. In the area's restaurants and markets, residents already find Mediterranean, Ethiopian, and Nepali food, and the Clarkston mayor told me he was intent on the city becoming an ethnic food destination. Given the community's diversity, the mayor's ambition seems fully achievable.

When I first met Rana and Fahia, I told them about Peace of Thread and its unique place in the community. I wasn't certain they had any interest in sewing, but I knew they would be welcome at Peace of Thread. I wanted them to meet Denise, her staff, and some of the threaders. The young women would determine for themselves whether they wanted to and could find the time to sew, given their work and study schedules. They recognized that the flexibility of the work and the supplementary income might be exactly what they needed. They asked about Denise, and then before we parted, they said something I still remember. Every day, they said, America surprised them because of its generous people.

Epilogue

On a rainy Sunday afternoon Emain, the refugee woman whose husband had been killed in Iraq, picked me up and drove the two of us to the refugee theaders' holiday party at Grace Village. Emain sparkled in an ankle-length dress embroidered with golden thread. Bracelets drew my eye from her shawl to her forearms and wrists.

We talked about the year we'd had, about her family—so far away— and about her son, Mamduah. He had just finished junior college, and in January he would start studying at Georgia State University, justifying the faith of the stranger who had set him on the path to a US education.

When we arrived at Grace Village, guests were ready with umbrellas to meet us at the car and protect us from the rain until we were inside. When I stepped into the main building, I immediately saw the gifts of Peace of Thread's generous mission. A richly decorated Christmas tree filled one corner of the room. Cloth-covered tables for eight filled two rooms, and in a third room, tables were laden with platters and bowls of food donated by volunteers. Many of the threaders had brought their children, and their voices filled the room with laughter. Two classically trained cellists from Celli, an Atlanta quartet, began to play Christmas music. The quartet had raised $10,000 for Peace of Thread in a six-hour "cellithon" earlier in the year.

Once everyone had arrived, Denise Smith asked the guests to join her in prayer. First she acknowledged each refugee woman by name, thanked her, and thanked the Lord.

"Thank you," she said, "for having brought these talented, beautiful women to us. Thank you for the opportunity to know them, to care about them, and for helping us empower them. Thank you for seeing us through hardships and for all the moments of joy we've experienced together."

Her words and tone of voice reflected the radiance of her expression, one of deep compassion for everyone there. Then her voice caught, and tears came to her eyes as she looked around the room and met the gaze of each of the threaders. Tears came to my eyes as well as I remembered the many hours I'd spent getting to know these extraordinary women.

Denise then introduced an artist who was ready with supplies of henna to decorate the hands of every woman who wanted to select a design. A masseuse was also waiting to give the refugee women a neck and shoulder massage.

After giving thanks and making the introductions, Denise invited everyone to dinner and suggested that each guest sit with someone she didn't know.

I sat with Rahima, a woman from Burma. She spoke very little English, but her children—a boy about eight years old and a girl aged five—served as her interpreters. They were eager to help their mother learn English and learn to drive, even though she had never driven in her home country and they didn't have a car. Already they were aware of the demands of their new home.

After a mixed feast of turkey and stuffing with side dishes that included hummus and spicy pickles, Denise took the floor again.

"I have an announcement," she said. "Today is Fatana's graduation. Thanks to the donations we received from the cellithon, we are able to sponsor a teaching program for ten refugee women. Fatana is the first one to complete the program."

Denise invited Fatana, a woman from Afghanistan, to the front of the room to receive a framed certificate with an embossed gold seal. Everyone clapped and cheered while the two women hugged. Then Denise continued.

"We also say thank you to Najah for being such a good teacher. Because of Najah's expert training, Fatana made three handbags on her own. Her easy-to-make bag, her medium-hard bag, and her hard bag all sold at our most recent show."

While the guests applauded again for these successes, Denise lifted a sewing bin and presented it to Fatana. Back in her seat, Fatana leaned over the bin, carefully opened its lid, and looked inside. Judging from the smile on her face, it seemed the box held all her wishes. In it were the sewing supplies she would need to work from home as well as her first sewing machine.

As I sat in the midst of this celebration, I looked around the room. Stephanie was serving the guests from a platter of cookies. April pulled a young child onto her lap. Nasima sat between a volunteer and a refugee woman interpreting for both of them and laughing with them. Like Denise, Fatana, and so many other threaders, I too felt thankful for the gifts all these women had given me—the gift of their stories, the gift of their friendship, and for the refugee women, the gift of gratitude for my country.

May you share these gifts as well.

Resources

Endnotes

Chapter 1: Transitions: A World of Possibilities

Bible Quote: New Living Translation of the Holy Bible

1. Leila Wahbeh is the subject of my first book, *Committee of One: Making a Difference One Life at a Time* (Atlanta: Matriarch Press, 2012).

2. A summary of this conflict is available at https://history.state.gov/milestones/1945-1952/arab-israeli-war; accessed 3-25-2019.

Chapter 2: Najah: Grateful to Be Home Again

Bible Quote: New Living Translation of the Holy Bible

1. Kurds are an ethnic and linguistic group that spans southeastern Turkey, northeastern Syria, northern Iraq, northwestern Iran, and southwestern Armenia. BBC News, "Who are the Kurds," October 31, 2017, http://www.bbc.com/news/world-middle-east-29702440; accessed 12-10-17.

2. Members of this ethnic group of Central Asia live in northern Iraq and other locations outside Turkmenistan. *Encyclopaedia Britannica*, "Turkmen People," https://www.britannica.com/topic/Turkmen-people; accessed 12-10-17.

3. In August 1990, Kuwait was attacked by Iraq. Central Intelligence Agency. *World Fact Book*, "Kuwait, Background," https://www.cia.gov/library/publications/resources/the-world-factbook/geos/ku.html; accessed 12-10-17.

4. The Iran-Iraq conflict lasted from 1980 to 1988. Iraq's leader at the time was Saddam Hussein. Woods KM, Murray W, Nathan EA, et al. *Saddam's Generals: Perspectives of the Iran-Iraq War*. Alexandria, Virginia: Institute for Defense Analyses, 2011.

5. In 1979, the Shah of Iran was deposed and went into exile. Ayatollah Khomeini became Iran's religious and political leader. BBC News, "Shah Flees Into Exile," http://news.bbc.co.uk/onthisday/hi/dates/stories/january/16/newsid_2530000/2530475.stm; accessed 12-5-17.

6. My friend Ibrahim, a devout Muslim and lawyer in Atlanta, educated me about Islamic marriage customs. According to Ibrahim, a suitor who does not ask to marry the oldest girl displays bad manners that undermine honor and dignity.

7. Ibrahim explained to me the subtlety of communication around a marriage proposal. Rather than say yes or no directly, a woman signals her feelings by her behavior. For example, if she blushes, her father or brother understand yes; if she turns away, the message is no. By leaving the decision to her brother, Najah conveyed her consent.

8. Ibrahim told me of another tradition for a woman getting married. She is draped

in gold, or gifted with gold by both families.

9. A man pays both an initial and a deferred dowry, Ibrahim explained, so that a woman is financially protected after a divorce or her husband's death.

10. In 1990, the United Nations imposed a financial and trade embargo on Iraq that lasted about 13 years. Global Policy Forum, "Sanctions Against Iraq," https://www. globalpolicy.org/previous-issues-and-debate-on-iraq/sanctions-against-iraq.html; accessed 12-5-17.

11. Ramadan is the Muslim month of fasting that ends with the celebration of Eid al-Fitr, a major Muslim holiday. Esposito, JL. *What Everyone Needs to Know About Islam*. New York: Oxford University Press, 2011.

12. A suburb of Atlanta a few miles from Clarkston.

13. The initialism for the Islamic State of Iraq and Syria, a global terrorist threat that has recruited fighters and spread violent extremist ideology. https://www.state. gov/s/seci/index.htm; accessed 12-10-17.

14. Kurdistan is an autonomous region of northern Iraq; see note 1 in this chapter.

Chapter 3: Denise and Art: Lifetime Guarantee
Bible Quote: King James Version
1. A version of the Bible, first published in 1971, that translates text into vernacular language with the intention of making the meaning more accessible. https://www. gotquestions.org/The-Living-Bible-TLB.html; accessed 1-11-18.

2. In some evangelical churches, a speaker invites congregants to come forward and pledge to follow Christ.
http://www.oneplace.com/ministries/regaining-lost-ground/read/articles/altar-calls--are-they-a-biblical-approach-14874.html; accessed 8-17-17.

3. A summary of this terrorist event is available at https://www.britannica.com/ event/September-11-attacks; accessed 1-11-18.

4. A dry spice mix of sesame seeds, thyme, and sumac. Bacon J, Fleetwood J. *The Complete Illustrated Food and Cooking of Africa and the Middle East*. London: Lorenz Books, 2009.

5. Damascus is about a two-hour drive from Beirut.

Chapter 4: Peace of Thread: Born in the USA
Bible Quote: New Living Translation of the Holy Bible

Chapter 5: Emain: Take Care of My Son
Bible Quote: King James Version
1. United Arab Emirates, a country on the Arabian Peninsula.
2. The head of a Muslim community. *Encyclopaedia Britannica*, "Imam," https:// www.britannica.com/topic/imam; accessed 12-15-17.

3. Currently around US$400. Conversion calculated at http://www.xe.com 1-14-18.

4. One of the refugee resettlement agencies in Atlanta.

Chapter 6: Denise's Circles: Comfort, Care, and Commitment

Bible Quote: New Living Translation of the Holy Bible

1. The Georgia Division of Family and Children Services oversees assistance such as food stamps, childcare, and medical needs. https://dfcs.georgia.gov/

2. In 2011, Campus Crusade for Christ changed its name to Cru. It remains a Christian ministry that has a presence in 190 countries. Cru, "History of Cru 2000–Present," https://www.cru.org/us/en/about/what-we-do/milestones.6.html; accessed 12-18-17.

3. Throughout the changes in her life Patsy maintained a relationship with her daughter. Today her daughter is married, has two grown sons, and is a social worker with a school system in Orlando, where she works with unwed mothers.

Chapter 7: Fahima: I Learned to Drive

Bible Quote: King James Version

1. Supporters credit Massoud with having envisioned a multiethnic Afghanistan. Many of his supporters are from the Panjshir River Valley in northern Afghanistan. https://www.npr.org/2011/09/09/140333732/in-afghanistan-assessing-a-rebel-leaders-legacy; accessed 12-13-17.

2. Mohammad served as both a translator (for written information) and an interpreter (for spoken information) during the joint US and British military intervention in Afghanistan, which began in 2001 and continues. *Encyclopaedia Britannica*, "Afghanistan War," https://www.britannica.com/event/Afghanistan-War; accessed 12-15-17.

3. Afghanis who worked directly with US Armed Forces as a translator or interpreter for at least 12 months can apply for a Special Immigrant Visa for permanent US residence. Up to 50 such visas are authorized for each fiscal year, except for 500 in both 2007 and 2008. US Department of State, Bureau of Consular Affairs, "Special Immigrant Visas (SIVs) for Iraqi and Afghan Translators/Interpreters," https://travel.state.gov/content/trvel/en/us-visas/immigrte/six-iraqi-afghan-translators-interpreters.html; accessed 12-15-17.

4. In 1989, Soviet forces withdrew from Afghanistan after a decade of guerrilla warfare. Then groups that had fought against Soviet forces turned against each other. *Encyclopaedia Britannica*, "Afghanistan War," https://www.britannica.com/event/Afghanistan-War#ref292841; accessed 1-9-18.

5. A loose-fitting, floor-length outer garment for women that also covers the head. It may cover the face as well and include a strip of lattice sewn in the area of the eyes. Glasse C. *The New Encyclopedia of Islam*. Lanham, MD: Rowman and

Littlefield, 2013.

6. IRC, one of the refugee resettlement agencies, has an office in Atlanta. Before arriving, refugees sign a promissory note agreeing to repay the US government the cost of airfare within 42 months. Westcott L, "A Brief History of Refugees Paying Back the US Government for Their Travel," *Newsweek*, 12/12/15, http://www.newsweek.com/brief-history-refugees-paying-back-us-government-their-travel-403241; accessed 12-15-17.

7. A city about 40 miles south of Clarkston.

8. Currently, application for naturalization costs a total of $725, including a background check cost referred to as a biometric fee. American Immigration Center, "How Much Does it Cost to Apply for US Citizenship," https://www.us-immigration.com/blog/how-much-does-it-cost-to-apply-for-us-citizenship; accessed 12-15-17.

Chapter 8: Nasima: The Price of Education
Bible Quote: King James Version

Chapter 9: Memphis: New Threaders, New Patterns
Bible Quote: New Living Translation of the Holy Bible

1. Lebanon has suffered decades of unrest since its independence in 1943. From 1976 to 2005, Syria occupied Lebanon, and after Syria's withdrawal, conflict with Israel occurred. Attacks and counterattacks in the summer of 2006 included the bombing of several locations in Syria. Central Intelligence Agency. *World Fact Book*, "Lebanon, Background," https://www.cia.gov/library/publications/resources/the-world-factbook/geos/le.html and BBC News. "2006: Lebanon War," http://news.bbc.co.uk/2/hi/middle_east/7381389.stm; both accessed 1-14-18.

2. *Encyclopaedia Britannica*, "Iraq War, 2003-2011," https://www.britannica.com/event/Iraq-War; accessed 1-14-18.

3. Filkins D. "At Least 11 Die in Car Bombing at Jordan's Embassy in Baghdad," August 7, 2003, *New York Times*, http://www.nytimes.com/2003/08/07/international/worldspecial/at-least-11-die-in-car-bombing-at-jordans-embassy.html; accessed 1-14-18.

4. Platt D. *Radical: Taking Back Your Faith from the American Dream*. Colorado Springs, CO: Multnomah Books, 2010.

5. A town about halfway between Somalia's capital, Mogadishu, and the country's border with Kenya.

6. Hogg AL. "Timeline: Somalia, 1991-2008." *The Atlantic*. December 2008. https://www.theatlantic.com/magazine/archive/2008/12/timeline-somalia-1991-2008/307190/; accessed 1-14-18.

7. Ifo is one of several refugee camps clustered around the city of Dadaab. Rawlence

B. *City of Thorns: Nine Lives in the World's Largest Refugee Camp*. New York: Picador, 2016.
8. About US$78 today. Conversion calculated at http://www.xe.com 1-14-18.

Chapter 10: Clarkston: One Square Global Mile
Bible Quote: New Living Translation of the Holy Bible
1. UNHCR names the 37 countries and those with the highest resettlement ceilings. See http://www.unhcr.org/en-us/information-on-unhcr-resettlement.html and http://www.unhcr.org/resettlement.html; both accessed 1-12-18.
2. For a look at life inside the Zaatari refugee camp, see the film *Salam Neighbor*.
3. Reported by the US State Department at https://www.state.gov/j/prm/ra/; accessed 12-18-17.
4. See http://www.uscripayments.org/; accessed 1-14-18.

New Living Translation
Holy Bible, New Living Translation copyright 2015 by Tyndale House Foundation. Tyndale House Publishers, Inc., Carol Stream, Illinois, 60188. All rights reserved.

King James Translation
Public Domain

Appendix

Facts about Clarkston, Georgia
• 10 miles northeast of Atlanta and 21 miles from Hartsfield-Jackson International Airport, one of the world's busiest
• Accessible by public transportation, both bus and rail
• About one-third of the population is foreign born
• Around three-fourths of the population is under the age of 40
• 60 languages are spoken by residents in just over one square mile
• Incorporated in 1882 and named for W. W. Clark, a railroad director, to acknowledge the city's network of rail connections
• One of the South's first suburban communities for workers commuting to Atlanta

For more information about the City of Clarkston, see http://clarkstonga.gov/.

Facts from the Coalition of Refugee Service Agencies (CRSA) for the Atlanta Area
• An umbrella group of refugee-serving organizations; some of these are local offices of international nonprofits

- ° Catholic Charities Atlanta
- ° CDF: A Collective Action Initiative
- ° Center for Pan-Asian Community Services
- ° Clarkston Community Center
- ° Friends of Refugees
- ° Georgia Asylum and Immigration Network (GAIN)
- ° Global Village Project
- ° International Rescue Committee Atlanta
- ° Jewish Family and Career Services
- ° The Lantern Project
- ° Latin American Association
- ° Lutheran Services of Georgia
- ° New American Pathways
- ° Refugee Coffee Company
- ° Refugee Women's Network
- ° Somali-American Community Center
- ° Tapestri
- ° Tekton Career Training
- ° World Relief Atlanta
- No state government funds programs specifically for refugees; funding comes from the federal level
- Before leaving the host country, refugees receive extensive background, security, and medical screenings—the most rigorous of any class of immigrants
- Refugees are of many faiths, including Christian, Muslim, Jewish, Hindu, and Buddhist
- Newly settled refugees learn English; in one recent year, CRSA members provided English-language training to nearly 3,000 clients
- CRSA members foster citizenship by making civics education available
- In 91 percent of refugee households in Georgia, family members are working and paying their own expenses within six months of arrival
- In Georgia, new immigrant business owners contribute about $3 billion in income (2013 data)
- Many of Georgia's refugees work in the state's largest industries, including poultry processing, manufacturing, warehousing, tourism, and hospitality

For more information about CRSA and Georgia's refugees, see:
https://crsageorgia.wordpress.com/.

Further Reading

Alexander J. *Chasing Chaos: My Decade In and Out of Humanitarian Aid*. New York: Random House, 2013.

Braun A. *The Promise of a Pencil: How an Ordinary Person Can Create Extraordinary Change*. New York: Scribner, 2014.

Capps R, Fix M. *Ten Facts about US Refugee Resettlement*. Washington, DC: Migration Policy Institute, 2015. https://www.migrationpolicy.org/research/ten-facts-about-us-refugee-resettlement; accessed 1-27-18.

Davis SC. *The Road from Damascus: A Journey Through Syria*. Seattle: Cune Press, 2003.

Holt PM. *Committee of One: Making a Difference One Life at a Time*. Atlanta: Matriarch Press, 2012.

Jurika-Owen D. *Ten Cultures, Twenty Lives: Refugee Life Stories*. Abilene, TX: Amaya Books, 2017.

Kidder T. *Mountains Beyond Mountains: The Quest of Dr. Paul Farmer, A Man Who Would Cure the World*. New York: Random House, 2003.

Lupton RD. *Toxic Charity: How Churches and Charities Hurt Those They Help (and How to Reverse It)*. New York: Harper-Collins, 2011.

Lupton RD. *Charity Detox: What Charity Would Look Like if We Cared About Results*. New York: Harper-Collins, 2015.

Maathai W. *Unbowed*. New York: Anchor Books, 2007.

Pipher M. *The Middle of Everywhere: Helping Refugees Enter the American Community*. Orlando, FL: Harcourt, 2002.

Prunier G. *Africa's World War: Congo, the Rwandan Genocide, and the Making of a Continental Catastrophe*. New York: Oxford University Press, 2009.

Rawlence B. *City of Thorns: Nine Lives in the World's Largest Refugee Camp*. New York: Picador, 2016.

Rush N. *The UN's Role in US Refugee Resettlement: A "benefit of the doubt" screening policy*. Washington, DC: Center for Immigration Studies, 2016. https://www.cis.org/sites/cis.org/files/rush-un-role-refugee_1.pdf; accessed 1-27-18.

St. John W. *Outcasts United: A Refugee Team, an American Town*. New York: Spiegel & Grau, 2009.

Shannon LJ. *A Thousand Sisters: My Journey into the Worst Place on Earth to be a Woman*. Berkeley, CA: Seal Press, 2010.

Stewart R. *The Places In Between*. New York: Houghton Mifflin Harcourt, 2007.

Zong J, Batalov J. *Refugees and Asylees in the United States*. Washington, DC: Migration Policy Institute, 2017. https://www.migrationpolicy.org/article/refugees-and-asylees-united-states; accessed 1-27-18.

For additional information about the worldwide refugee issue and refugee resettlement, consult the website of the United Nations High Commissioner for Refugees: http://www.unhcr.org/en-us/.

For additional information about refugee and other humanitarian issues as addressed by the US government, consult factsheets and other releases on the website of the US Department of State:

https://www.state.gov/j/prm/releases/factsheets/.

Acknowledgments

No words can I find to thank the women and men who are the subjects of this book. Their patience, forbearance, and honesty lasted over the three years it has taken to complete this story.

Thanks to my close friends here in Atlanta, who may feel they've written every page with me, I've received support, laughter, and companionship. Barbara Barnes, Marianne Betts, Carol Heeren, Sue-Ann Soloway, and JoAnn Weiss made sure I had fun and frolic to balance the sadness of the stories I heard. Leila Wahbeh set me in motion all those years ago in Amman, Jordan, by putting the refugee story in front of me in all its complexity. She taught me that while we can't do everything, we can do something.

Diane Hawkins-Cox, an editor of my first book and a dear friend of long standing, introduced me to my current editor, and now friend whose magic with words gave me the fortitude to keep on. My gratitude for her steadfastness and unflappability is immeasurable.

I was made welcome at the Alif Institute for Arab education and culture by Director Angela Khoury and staff Alta Schwartz and Zainab Al Qasiri. From the Institute sprang friendships with them and with Fahed Abu-Akel and Ibrahim Awad. All of these new friends have huge hearts and political intelligence.

Without the patience and kindness of interpreters Iman Hadeed and Chantal Mucyo, important sections of Emain's and Aminata's stories would be missing. These interpreters have my respect for their linguistic abilities and my appreciation for their friendship.

My writing friends—Ruth Asher, Peggy Mooers, and Brian Jory—have celebrated and lamented with me as situations have demanded. We've traveled a long and sometimes bumpy road together. May their faith in my talent and their own remain unshakable.

I owe so much to my beloved daughter Gerryll, whose humor and encouragement never fail to boost my spirits. She has made life's losses much easier to bear.

Thanks to Global Giving for compiling the quotations about refugees on the first page of this book and to Tyndale House Publishers for Bible citations in the New Living Translation.

Index

Note: Refugees are listed by first name only.

A

Abu-Akel, Fahed, 3, 125
Adventures in Missions, 73
Afghan, 14, 79-80, 82, 84, 118
Afghanistan, 45-46, 70, 75, 79-82, 84-85, 88-90, 113, 117-118
Ahdebahng, 46
Ahmed, 20-26, 41-42, 45
Aleppo, Syria, 8, 104-105, 127
Aley, Lebanon, 35, 37, 39, 91, 94
Al-Fatiha, 22
American Immigration Center, 118
Aminata, 101, 125
Amman, Jordan, 13, 23-24, 125, 128
Arab Army, 18
Arabic, 2, 14, 41, 60, 68, 89, 94, 104, 108
Arab-Israeli War, 13
artisan threaders, 9, 12-13, 16, 20, 40, 43, 45-48, 53-54, 62, 64-65, 67, 69, 73, 76-77, 84, 91, 95, 97, 101, 103, 111-113, 118
Athens, Georgia, 69
Atlanta, Georgia, 2-3, 10, 13-14, 25, 31-32, 34-35, 39, 42, 47, 60-61, 73, 81, 84, 90, 95, 97, 101, 106, 108, 110, 112, 115-118, 121-123, 125
Atlanta Decorative Arts Center (ADAC), 42-43, 76
Auburn University, 76

B

Baada, 46
Backyard Humanity Movement, 7-8
Baghdad, Iraq, 55, 69, 119
BBC, 90, 115, 119
Beirut, Lebanon, 2, 35-37, 91, 94-95, 116
Berry College, 63
Bible, 8, 11, 27-29, 32, 64, 72, 94-95, 115-119, 125
bilingual, 14, 97
Biloxi, Mississippi, 93
Bloom Township, Ohio, 30
Boulder, Colorado, 31
Burchik, Erin, 3, 47, 76
Burma, 113

C

California State Polytechnic University, 72
Campus Crusade for Christ, 72, 93, 117
Carroll, Andrea, 76

Catholic Charities, 95, 100, 121
CDF: A Collective Action Initiative, 121
Center for Pan-Asian Community Services, 121
Charlotte, North Carolina, 33
Christian, 13, 19, 68, 103, 117, 122
churches, 52, 95, 116, 123
Clarkston, Georgia, 2, 6, 9, 13-14, 17, 25, 33, 39, 42, 47, 49-51, 53-54, 60, 68-70, 76-77, 79, 81, 83, 104-106, 108-111, 116, 118-119, 121, 128
Clarkston Community Center, 77, 121
Coalition of Refugee Service Agencies (CRSA), 121-122
Columbus, Ohio, 27
Congolese, 14, 75, 94, 101-102, 123
Costa Rica, 33, 73

D

Dadaab, Kenya, 98, 119
Dagahaley (refugee camp), 98
Damascus, Syria, 8, 36, 116, 123, 127
Decatur, Georgia, 25
Democratic Republic of the Congo, 75, 94, 101-102, 123
Denver, Colorado, 31
Department of Homeland Security, 106
Deuteronomy 10:18-19, 39
Deuteronomy 14:28-29, 62
dishdasha, 18
dowry, 21, 85, 101, 116
Druze, 37, 94
Dubai, United Arab Emirates, 57

E

education, 9, 38, 45, 55, 61, 66, 70, 84-85, 89, 100, 106, 109-112, 118, 122, 125
effendi, 18
Eid al-Fitr, 24, 85, 116
Einstein, Albert, 1
Emain, 9, 45, 50, 55, 112, 117, 125
Emory University, 84, 90
English, 14, 25, 34, 39, 45, 51, 60-61, 70, 72, 76-77, 79, 84, 89, 97, 99, 101, 104, 106, 109, 113, 122
Entebbe, Uganda, 94
Eureka, California, 72
Exodus 23:9, 13

F

Fahia, 104, 106, 108-111

Fahima, 9, 79, 82-83, 117
Farsi, 89
Fatima, 97-99
Flanders, Denise, 49, 52, 66, 68-70
Freshta, 46
Friends of Refugees, 121

G
Gainesville, Georgia, 73
Georgia Asylum and Immigration Network
(GAIN), 105, 121
Georgia Division of Family and Children
Services (Family and Children Services), 82, 117
Georgia Perimeter College, 60, 66
Georgia State University, 112
Germany, 25, 35-36, 86
Ghazni, Afghanistan, 85
Global Village Project, 121
Grace Fellowship Church, 32-34, 47, 51-54,
62-63, 68, 76
Grace Village, 54, 77, 112

H
habiba, 97, 100
Habitat for Humanity, 100
Hagadera (refugee camp), 98
halal, 81
handbags, 10, 13, 42-43, 45, 50, 68, 75-76, 81,
103, 113
headscarf, 49, 68
Hebrews 13:1-3, 84
Hernando, Mississippi, 91, 93, 102
hijab, 17, 49, 68, 86
Hindi, 89
Hoffman, Buddy, 32
housing, 97, 99, 110
Hussein, Saddam, 57, 115

I
Ifo (refugee camps), 98, 119
International Committee of the Red Cross, 35,
106
International Organization for Migration, 24,
108
International Rescue Committee (IRC), 81,
108-111, 118, 121
interpreters, 14, 113, 118, 125
Intertwined Candles, 54
Iran-Iraq War, 19, 115
Iraq, 14, 17-19, 22-24, 36, 39, 41, 46, 55-61,
65, 75-76, 81, 93-95, 112, 115-116, 118-119
Isaiah 16:2-4, 17
Islamic law, 21
Israel, 18, 118

J
Jeremiah 22:3, 104
Jewish Family and Career Services, 121
Johnson, Barbara, 77

K
Kabul, Afghanistan, 79-81, 83-86, 89-90
Kabul TV, 90
Kabul University, 89
Khomeini, Ayatollah, 115
Khoury, Angela, 2, 125
King, Bobby, 3, 109
King James Bible, 8, 28, 116-119
Kurds, 19, 26, 115-116
Kurtun, Somalia, 97
Kuwait, 19, 23, 115

L
Lamb, Renee, 49, 91, 96
Lantern Project, 53-54, 121
Latin American Association, 121
Lebanon, 2, 13, 35-39, 42, 49, 64, 68, 77, 91,
94-95, 116, 118-119
Lebanon Bag, 49
Leviticus 19:33-34, 27
Lilburn, Georgia, 32, 75
Lisha, 65-66
Living Bible, 8, 28
London, England, 63, 116
Louna, 46
Love Your Enemies, 63
Luaa, 55-59
Luke 10:36, 91
Lutheran Services of Georgia, 122

M
Mamduah, 56-57, 59-60, 112
Manassas, Virginia, 83
Marbut, Stephanie, 32, 71, 100
Massoud, Ahmad, 79, 117
Matthew 25: 3-45, 11
Meltzer, Hannah, 77
Memphis, Tennessee, 9, 14, 49, 77, 91, 95-97,
99-100, 102-103, 118
Merkel, Angela 8
Miami, Florida, 29-30, 74
Middle East, 14, 34, 36, 64, 68, 94, 116, 119
militias, 23, 58-59, 101
missionaries, 72
missions, 37, 73, 93-94
Mohammad, 79-83, 117
mosque, 80-81, 89, 99
Muslim, 17, 36, 49, 68, 88, 93, 104, 115-117,
122
Myanmar, 14

N
Najah, 9, 17-18, 20-21, 32, 41, 45, 50, 113, 115-116
Nasima, 9, 84-85, 87-90, 113, 118
New American Pathways, 122
New York City, 34-35
North Kurdistan, 26
Nuam, 48

O
Obama, Michelle, 103
Operation Mobilization, 35-36, 38, 91
Orlando, Florida, 31, 62, 117, 123

P
Pakistan, 81, 85, 87
Palestine, 18
Palestinian, 13, 19
Panjshir River Valley, Afghanistan, 79-80, 117
Peace of Thread, 2-3, 7-10, 13-15, 17, 39, 45-47, 49-55, 61-62, 64-66, 69-70, 72-77, 79, 83-84, 90-91, 95, 97-98, 100, 102-104, 110-112, 117, 128
Peace of Thread Northeast, 49
Phil Donahue Show, 31
Pitts, Mary Lynn, 76, 100
post-traumatic stress disorder (PTSD), 66
President Obama, 61
Punta Gorda, Florida, 74

Q
Qur'an, 21-22, 101

R
Rahima, 113
Ramadan, 24, 61, 116
Rana, 104, 106, 108-111
Refugee Coffee Company, 122
refugee camps, 13, 106, 119
Refugee Women's Network, 122
refugees, 1-3, 6, 8, 13-15, 17, 25, 34, 42, 51-54, 62, 64, 66, 69, 72-73, 75-77, 91, 95, 98-99, 104-106, 108-110, 118, 121-125, 128
Roberts, Patsy, 78
Russell, Melanie, 77
Russia, 20, 86

S
Santa Maria, California, 31
Sapidah, 70, 72
schools, 33, 83, 85, 88
SCM Medical Missions 9
sewing, 2, 13-14, 25, 41-43, 45, 49-51, 54, 60-62, 66, 68-69, 76-77, 82-83, 85, 95, 100,
102, 111, 113
sewing machines, 13, 41-43, 62, 76-77, 95
Sharia law, 89
Shia, 19, 57-59
Smith, Art, 29
Smith, Caleb, 30-31, 33
Smith, Danielle, 31, 33, 41
Smith, Denise, 2-3, 9, 13-14, 17, 25, 27-39, 41-43, 45-47, 49-55, 60-70, 72-73, 75-77, 81-84, 91, 95, 97, 100, 102, 104, 110-113, 116-117, 128
Smith, Jesse, 31-33, 38, 68, 75
Somali, 14, 34
Somali-American Community Center, 122
souk, 36
St. Jude Children's Research Hospital, 77, 103
Sunni, 18-19, 23, 57-58

T
Taliban, 79-80, 90
Tapestri, 122
Tekton, 53, 121
Terry, Edward (Mayor), 2, 108
Turkish TV, 90
Turkmen, 19, 115

U
United Arab Emirates, 117
United Nations High Commissioner for Refugees (UNHCR), 105, 124
United Nations (UN), 60, 98, 105, 116, 123-124
United Nations World Food Program (WFP), 105
United States, 14, 24-26, 55, 60, 75, 80-81, 84, 88-90, 93-94, 99, 104-106, 124
University of Memphis College of Art, 103

V
Vancouver, Washington, 74
volunteers, 2-3, 13-14, 17, 35, 37, 43, 45-47, 49-50, 54, 62, 64, 66, 69, 72-73, 75-77, 90, 94-95, 97, 103, 110, 112, 128

W
Wahbeh, Leila, 13, 115, 125, 128
Wertz, Dorothy Fonde, 76
Wheaton, Illinois, 30
World Race, 72-73
World Relief, 70, 84, 122
World Trade Center, 34

Z
Zaatari (refugee camp), 105-106, 119
Zawaideh, Rita 8-9
Zechariah 7:9-10, 55

Cune Press

Cune Press was founded in 1994 to publish thoughtful writing of public importance. Our name is derived from "cuneiform." (In Latin *cuni* means "wedge.")

In the ancient Near East the development of cuneiform script—simpler and more adaptable than hieroglyphics—enabled a large class of merchants and landowners to become literate. Clay tablets inscribed with wedge-shaped stylus marks made possible a broad intermeshing of individual efforts in trade and commerce.

Cuneiform enabled scholarship to exist and art to flower, and created what historians define as the world's first civilization. When the Phoenicians developed their sound-based alphabet, they expressed it in cuneiform.

The idea of Cune Press is the democratization of learning, the faith that rarefied ideas, pulled from dusty pedestals and displayed in the streets, can transform the lives of ordinary people. And it is the conviction that ordinary people, trusted with the most precious gifts of civilization, will give our culture elasticity and depth—a necessity if we are to survive in a time of rapid change.

Aswat: Voices from a Small Planet (a series from Cune Press)

Looking Both Ways — Pauline Kaldas
Stage Warriors — Sarah Imes Borden
Stories My Father Told Me — Helen Zughaib & Elia Zughaib

Syria Crossroads (a series from Cune Press)

Leaving Syria — Bill Dienst & Madi Williamson
Visit the Old City of Aleppo — Khaldoun Fansa
The Plain of Dead Cities — Bruce McLaren
Steel & Silk — Sami Moubayed
Syria - A Decade of Lost Chances — Carsten Wieland
The Road from Damascus — Scott C. Davis
A Pen of Damascus Steel — Ali Ferzat
White Carnations — Musa Rahum Abbas

Bridge Between the Cultures (a series from Cune Press)

Empower a Refugee — Patricia Martin Holt
Biblical Time Out of Mind — Tom Gage, James A. Freeman
Turning Fear Into Power — Linda Sartor
The Other Side of the Wall — Richard Hardigan
A Year at the Edge of the Jungle — Frederic Hunter
Curse of the Achille Lauro — Reem al-Nimer

Patricia Martin Holt raised three children, worked as a law firm administrator, and served in management positions for numerous professional and civic organizations before opening a management consulting business of her own. When her husband, a hydrologist, accepted a position in Amman, Jordan, she closed her business and joined him on a new adventure.

In exploring her new culture, Holt met Leila Wahbeh and saw the difference one purposeful woman made in the lives of thousands of refugees in camps in and around Amman. Her story became the subject of Holt's first book, *Committee of One*, for which Holt was named a Georgia Author of the Year and awarded an Independent Publishers Association Bronze Medal. Back in the States, Holt's sustained interest in refugee lives drew her to Clarkston, Georgia, a hub of refugee resettlement near her home.

In Clarkston, she met Denise Smith, a woman whose faith and personal experience of loss compelled her to find a way to help refugee women rebuild their lives. Smith founded Peace of Thread, a handbag company for which refugee women manufacture one-of-a-kind products. Empower a Refugee tells the story of this remarkable enterprise and of its founder, volunteers, and unique employees. When not writing, Holt is in her fine craft studio, working in clay.

Peace of Thread welcomes public participation. For more information: www.peaceofthread.com / .org